ESSAYS ÆSTHETICAL

BY

GEORGE H. CALVERT

BOSTON
LEE AND SHEPARD, PUBLISHERS
NEW YORK
LEE, SHEPARD, AND DILLINGHAM
1875

RIVERSIDE, CAMBRIDGE:
STEREOTYPED AND PRINTED BY
H. O. HOUGHTON AND COMPANY.

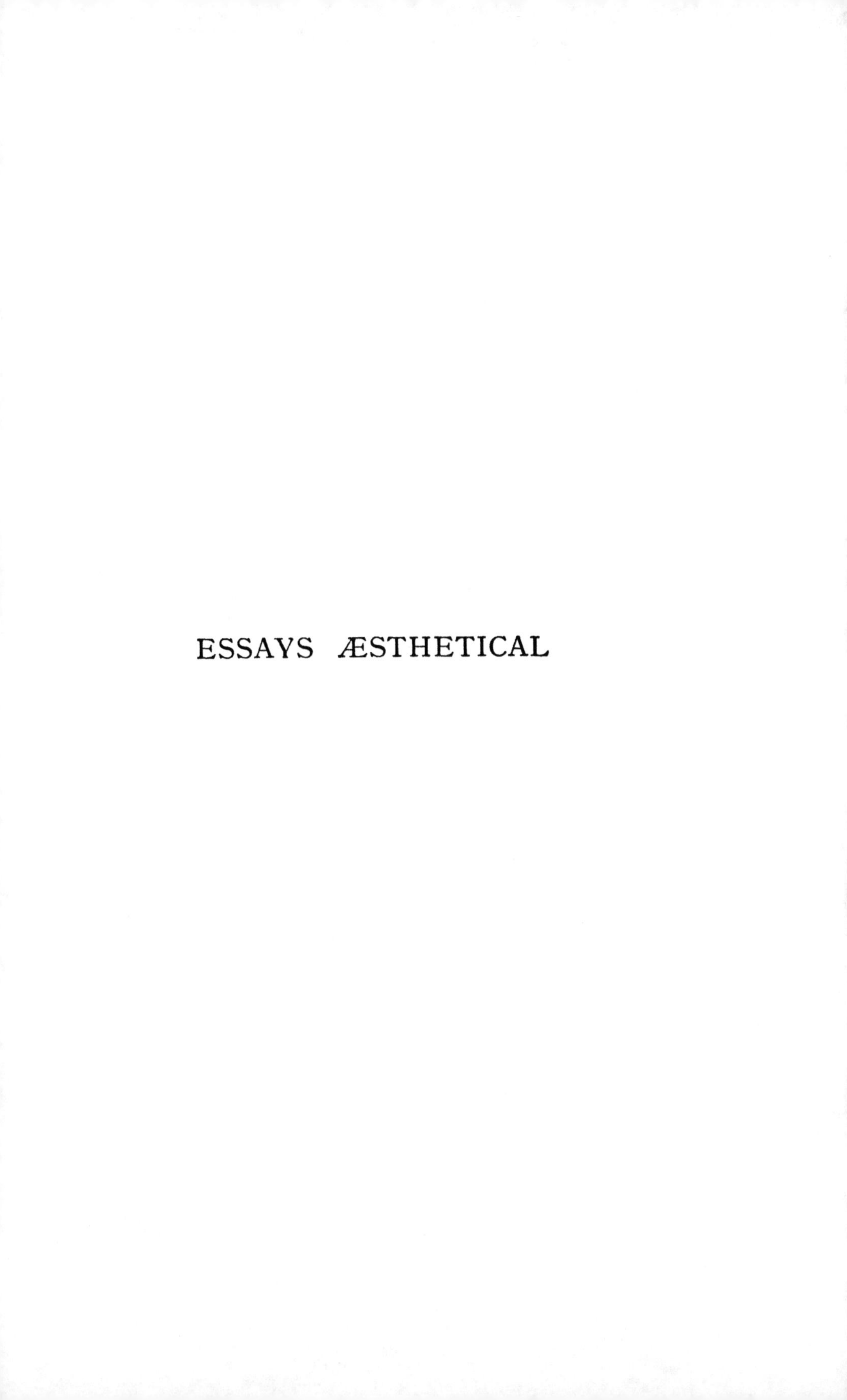

ESSAYS ÆSTHETICAL

CONTENTS.

ESSAYS ÆSTHETICAL.

I.

THE BEAUTIFUL.

THE Beautiful is one of the immortal themes. It cannot die; it grows not old. On the same day with the sun was beauty born, and its life runs parallel with the path of that great beautifier. As a subject for exposition, it is at once easy and difficult: easy, from the affluence of its resources; difficult, from the exactions which its own spirit makes in the use of them.

Beauty — what is it? To answer this question were to solve more than one problem. Shall we attempt what has been so often attempted and never fully achieved? Such attempts are profitable. What though we reach not the very heart of the mystery, we may get near enough to hearken to the throb of its power, and our minds will be nerved by the approximation.

To him who has the gift to feel its presence, nature teems with beauty. Whithersoever the senses reach, whenever emotion kindles, wherever the mind seeks food for its finer appetites, there is beauty. It expects us at the dawn ; it is about us, "an hourly neighbor," through the day ; at night it looks down on us from star-peopled immensities. Glittering on green lawns, glowing in sunsets, flashing through storm-clouds, gilding our wakeful hours, irradiating sleep, it is ever around, within us, eager to sweeten our labors, to purify our thoughts. Nature is a vast treasure-house of beauty, whereof the key is in the human heart.

But many are the hearts that have never opened far enough to disclose the precious key enfolded in their depths. Whole peoples are at this moment ignorant that they live amid such wealth. As with them now, so in the remote primitive times of our own race, before history was, nature was almost speechless to man. The earth was a waste, or but a wide hunting ground or pasturage ; and human life a round of petty animal circles, scarcely sweeping beyond the field of the senses ; until there gradually grew up the big-eyed Greek and the deep-souled Hebrew. Then, through creative thought, — that is, thought quickened and exalted by an inward thirst for the beautiful, — one little corner of Europe became radiant, and the valley of Tempe and the wooded glens of Parnassus shone for the first time on the vision of men; for their eyes — opened from long sleep by inward stirring — were become as mirrors, and gave back the light of nature:

> "Auxiliar light
> Came from their minds, which on the setting sun
> Bestowed new splendor."[1]

And man, heated by the throbs of his swelling heart, made gods after his own image, — forms of such life and power and harmony that the fragments of them, spared by time, are still guarded as faultless models of manhood. And the vales and groves and streams were peopled with beauteous shapes. And the high places were crowned with temples which, in their majestic purity, look as though they had been posited there from above by heavenly hands. And by the teemful might of sculptors and painters and poets the dim past was made resurgent and present in glorious transfiguration. And the moral law was grasped at by far-reaching philosophies. In this affluence of genial

[1] Wordsworth.

activity so much truth was embodied in so much beauty, that by the products of the Greek mind even the newer, the deeper, the wiser Christian spirit is still instructed, still exalted.

In Asia, too, a chosen people early made a revelation of the beautiful. The Hebrews were introspective. At once ardent and thoughtful, passionate and spiritual, their vigorous natures were charged with fiery materials for inward conflicts. Out of the secret chambers of troubled souls their poets and prophets sent forth cries of despair and of exultation, of expostulation and self-reproach, that ever find an echo in the conscience-smitten, sorrow-laden bosom of man. The power and wisdom of God they saw as no other ancient people had seen them. In the grandeurs and wonders of creation they could behold the being and the might and the goodness of the Creator. The strong, rich hearts of their seers yearned for a diviner life, in the deep, true consciousness they felt that there can be peace and joy to man only through reconcilement with God. And feeling their own unworthiness and impurity, as well as that of their people, they uttered their spiritual desires, and their aspirations and disappointments and indignations and humiliations, in strains that make their great writings sound like one long, impassioned, rhythmic wail through the bars of a dungeon. Gloomy, wrathful, and intense, their utterances are grand and pathetic and sublime ; but the beautiful plays through them, and gilds their highest points as the white crests do the billows of a black, tempestuous sea.

Save these two, no other nations of antiquity, except the Hindoos, seem to have had more than a superficial susceptibility to the beautiful. The Romans learnt the arts from the Greeks, whom they imitated, at a wide distance, in poetry as well as in sculpture and architecture. The remnants of art found in the valley of the Nile prove the Egyptians to have had the germ without the vitality to unfold it. In the literature of the Hindoos there are currents of pure poetry and of biblical depth. In passing down from ancient to modern times the Persians and the Arabians light the long way with scintillations from the beautiful.

The ugly semi-barbarian darkness of the Middle Ages in Europe was first broken by the light that shone from the spires of Gothic cathedrals in the eleventh century. About the twelfth century the German mind was further illuminated by that mysterious, visionary, titanic, Teutonic epic, the Niebelungen Lied; and a little later appeared the troubadours in the south of Europe and the minnesingers (love-singers) in Germany. Next came Dante and Giotto in Italy, then Chaucer in England; so that by the end of the fourteenth century, poetry and the arts, the offspring of the beautiful, — and who can have no other parentage, — had established themselves in the modern European mind, and have since, with varying vigor of life, upheld themselves among Christian nations. To these they are now confined. In the most advanced of Mahometan and heathen peoples sensibility to beauty is hardly awakened, and among savages it seems scarcely to exist, so deeply is it dormant.

Thus to indicate when and by whom the beautiful has been recognized will further us in the endeavor to learn wherein consists that which, enriching the world of man so widely and plenteously, is deeply enjoyed by so few.

Were the beautiful, like size and shape and strength and nimbleness, cognizable by intellectual perception, even the Hottentot would get to know something of it in the forest, along with the grosser qualities of trees and valleys. Were it liable to be seized by the discursive and ratiocinative intellect, the most eminent statesman or lawyer or general would excel too in the capacity to appreciate beauty; the Roman would have shone in arts as in arms; the Spartan would not have been so barren where the Athenian was so prolific. But beauty is *felt*, not intellectually apprehended or logically deduced. Its presence is acknowledged by a gush from the soul, by a joyous sentimental recognition, not by a discernment of the understanding. When we exclaim, How beautiful! there is always emotion, and delightful, expansive, purifying emotion. Whence this mysterious cleansing thrill? Thence, that the recognition of beauty ever denotes, ever springs out of, sympathy with the creative spirit whence all things have their being.

The beautiful, then, is not subject to the intellect. We cannot demonstrate or coldly discover it; we cannot weigh or measure it. Further to illustrate this position: we do not see with our outward eye any more than we do with spectacles. The apparent ocular apparatus is but the passive, unconscious instrument to transmit images thrown through it upon a fine interior fibre, the optic nerve; and even this does not take cognizance of the object, but is only another conductor, carrying the image still farther inward, to the intellectual nerves of the brain; and not until it reaches them do we see the object, not until then is its individuality and are its various physical qualities, size, shape, etc., apprehended. And now the intellect itself becomes a conductor, transmitting still deeper inward to the seat of emotion the image of the object; and not until it reaches that depth is its beauty recognized.

In all her structures and arrangements Nature is definite, precise, and economical. In subdivision of labor she is minute and absolute, providing for every duty its special exclusive agent. In the mind there is as severe a sundering of functions as in the body, and the intellect can no more encroach upon or act for the mental sensibilities than the stomach can at need perform the office of the heart, or the liver that of the lungs. True, no ripe results in the higher provinces of human life can be without intimate alliance between the mental sensibilities and the intellect; nevertheless they are in essence as distinct from one another as are the solar heat and the moisture of the earth, without whose constant coöperation no grain or fruit or flower can sprout or ripen.

We live not merely in a world of material facts, and of objects and things cognizable through the senses, but also in a spiritual world. We live not only in presence of visible creation, but in presence of the invisible Creator. With the creation we are in contact through the intellect. Knowledge of all objects and the qualities of objects that are within reach of the senses; distance and other material relations; the bonds of cause and effect and of analogy, that bind all created things in countless multiplicity of subtle relations,—these the intellect gathers in its grasp. But with the Creator we are in communication only through feeling. The presence, the existence of God cannot by pure intellect be demonstrated: it must be felt in order to be proved. The mass of objects and relations presented to us in nature the intellect can learn, count, and arrange; but the life that incessantly permeates the whole and every part, the spirit that looks out from every object and every fact,—of the range and pitch of whose power we have a faint token in the tornado and the earthquake,—of this divine essence we should not have even an intimation through the intellect alone. Not chemists, astronomers, mechanicians have uttered the deepest thoughts about God, but prophets and poets: not Davys, but Coleridges; not Herschels, but Wordsworths. It is a common belief, indeed, that men addicted to the exact sciences are rather wanting than otherwise in power to appreciate the invisible, a belief pungently embodied by Wordsworth in the lines, —

> "Physician art thou? one all eyes,
> Philosopher! a fingering slave,
> One that would peep and botanize
> Upon his mother's grave?"

This is as much under the mark as is above it that saying of some one, "An undevout astronomer is mad." A man's being endowed with rare mathematical talent is no cause why he should or should not be devout. His gifts to weigh and measure the stars are purely intellectual; and nature being seldom profuse upon one individual, — as she was upon Pascal and Newton, — the presumption as to an astronomer, of whom we know nothing, would be that what may be termed his emotive appreciation of stars and stellar systems is probably not so full as his intellectual. And no amount or quality of intellectual insight can supply or compensate a want of sensibility. No matter how many hundreds of millions of miles he may pierce into space, he has still to do with the visible and calculable. But religion is the putting of the human mind in relation with the invisible, the incalculable. A man gets no nearer to God through a telescope than through a microscope, and no nearer through either than through the naked eye. Who cannot recognize the divine spirit in the hourly phenomena of nature and of his own mind will not be helped by the differential calculus, or any magnitude or arrangement of telescopic lenses.

That we ever live not only in a material, but also in a spiritual world, can be easily apprehended without at all entangling ourselves in the web-work of metaphysics. The least of our acts or motions, is it not always preceded by a thought, a volition, a something intangible, invisible? All that we voluntarily do is, must be, an offspring of mind. The waving of the hand is never a simple, it is a compound process: mind and body, spirit and matter, concur in it. The visible, corporeal movement is but the outward expression of an inward, incorporeal movement. And so in all our acts and motions, from birth till death; they issue out of the invisible within us; they are feelings actualized, thoughts embodied. The embodiment is perishable, the source of it imperishable. It is not a recondite, super-subtle, metaphysical or psychological postulate, it is a palpable, and may be and ought to be a familiar fact, that each one of us is ruled by the eternal and invisible within us.

Now, just as our words and deeds and movements stand to our mind, as being the utterance and embodiment of that, so do we stand towards Deity, being the utterance and embodiment of the divine thought and will. As all our doings are but exhibitions of our minds, so ourselves are manifestations of God. Through all things shines the eternal soul. The more perfect the embodiment, the more translucent is the soul; and when this is most transparent, making the body luminous with the fullness of its presence, there is beauty, which may be said to be the most intense and refined incarnation and exhibition of the divine spirit.

Behind and within every form of being is immanent the creative power; and thence, in proportion as this power discloses itself, is object, act, or emotion beautiful. Thus is beauty always spiritual, a revelation more or less clear of the creative spirit. Hence our emotion in presence of the truly beautiful, which calms and exalts us. Hence evil never is, cannot be, beautiful: the bad is, must be, ugly. Evil consists in the deficiency of the divine creative spirit, whose fullness gives, is, beauty. Evil is imperfection, unripeness, shapelessness, weakness in, or opposition to, the creative spirit. Evil is life that is unhealthy, short-coming. Wherever there is full, unperverted life, there is, there must be, beauty. The beautiful blossoms on every stem of unpoisoned power. The sap of sound life ever molds itself into forms of beauty.

But however rich the exhibition of the divine soul, however glowing with perfection the form, however noble the act and pure the feeling, the richness, the perfection, the nobleness, the purity will be lost on us, unless within us there be sympathy with the spirit whence they flow. Only by spirit can spirit be greeted.

Thus beauty only becomes visible — I might say only becomes actual — by the fire kindled through the meeting of a perfection out of us and an inward appetite therefor. And it is the flaming of this fire, thus kindled, that lights up to us the whole world wherein we live, the inward and the outward. This fire unlighted, and on the face of nature there is darkness, in our own minds there is darkness. For though all nature teems with the essence and the outward mold of beauty, to the unkindled mind beauty is no more present then was Banquo's ghost to the guests of Macbeth. Macbeth's individual conscience made him see the ghost; nay, by a creative potency summoned it: and so is beauty created there where, without what I may call the æsthetic conscience, it no more exists than do the glories of Titian and Claude to the affectionate spaniel who follows his master into a picture-gallery. To the quadruped, by the organic limitation of his nature, dead forever is this painted life. By the organic boundlessness of *his* nature, man can grasp the life of creation in its highest, its finest, its grandest manifestations; and from these beauty is indivisible. Wherever the divine energy is most subtle and expressive, there glows ever, in its celestial freshness, the beautiful.

Beauty is the happiest marriage between the invisible and the visible. It may be termed the joyfullest look of God. Blessed is he who can watch and reflect this radiant look. The faculties of such a one become fortified by creative influx. Through the exquisite shock of the beautiful he reaps an accession of mental magnetism. Thus through the beautiful we commune the most directly with the divine ; and, other things being equal, to the degree that men respond to, are thrilled by, this vivacity of divine presence, as announced by the beautiful, to that degree are they elevated in the scale of being.

Nature being minute and absolute in subdivision of function, the law of severalty and independence — than which there is no law more important and instructive — pervades creation. Thence the intellectual, the religious, the true, the good, cannot interchange functions. A man may be sincerely religious and do little for others, as is seen in anchorites, and in many one-sided people, of Christian as well as of Mahometan parentage, who are not anchorites. A man may be immensely intellectual and not value truth. But neither a man's intellect, nor his preference for truth, nor his benevolent nor his religious sentiment, can yield its best fruit without the sunshine of the beautiful. Sensibility to the beautiful — itself, like the others, an independent inward power — stands to each one of them in a relation different from that which they hold one to the other. The above and other faculties *indirectly* aid one the other, and to the complete man their united action is needed; but feeling for the beautiful *directly* aids each one, aids by stimulating it, by expanding, by purifying.

To the action of every other faculty this one gives vividness and grace. It indues each with privilege of insight into the *soul* of the object which it is its special office to master. By help of sensibility to the beautiful we have inklings of the essence of things, we sympathize with the inward life that molds the outward form. Hence men highly gifted with this sensibility become creative, in whatever province of work they strive; and no man in any province is truly creative except through the subtle energy imparted to him by this sensibility, this competence to feel the invisible in the visible.

The idea is the invisible; the embodiment thereof is the visible. Hence the beautiful is always ideal; that is, it enfolds, embraces, represents, with more or less success, the idea out of which springs the object it illuminates: it brilliantly enrobes a germinal essence. It is thus a sparkling emanation out of the Infinite, and it leads us thither whence it has come.

Sensibility to the beautiful is thus the light of the whole mind, illuminating its labors. Without it we work in the dark, and therefore feebly, defectively. Infer thence the immensity of its function. Hereby it becomes the chief educator of men and of man ; and where its teaching has not been conspicuous, there no elevation has been reached. The Greeks and the Hebrews would not have been so deeply, so greatly, so feelingly known to us, would not have been the pioneers and inspirers of European civilization, would not have lived on through thousands of years in the minds of the highest men, had they not, along with their other rare endowments, possessed, in superior, in unique quality, this priceless gift of sensibility to the beautiful. Through this gift Shakespeare is the foremost man of England, and through it has done more than any other man to educate and elevate England. Because the Italians of the fourteenth and fifteenth centuries were so rich in this gift, therefore it is that Italy is still a shrine to which the civilized world makes annual pilgrimage.

The supreme function of this sensibility is to develop, to educate, to chasten the highest faculties, our vast discourse of reason, our unselfish aspiration, our deep instinct of truth, our capacious love. To educate these is its cardinal duty, and lacking this they remain uneducated. But its beneficent influence is felt likewise in the less elevated of our efforts. The man who makes shoes, as well as he who makes laws and he who makes poems; the builder of houses, with the builder of theologies or cosmogonies; the engineer, as well as the artist, all work under the rays of this illuminator; and, other things being equal, he excels all others on whose work those rays shine with the most sustained and penetrative force.

> " 'T is the eternal law,
> That first in beauty shall be first in might." [1]

In short, whatever the mental gift, in order to get from that gift its best fruit, the possessor must be incited, upborne, enlightened, inspired by the ideal, which burns as a transfiguring flame in his mind, and throws thence its joyful light with every blow of his hand.

All good work is more or less creative, that is, a co-working with the eternal mind; and

[1] Keats.

work is good and productive in proportion to the intensity of this coöperation. Why is it that we so prize a fragment of Phidias, a few lines traced by Raphael? Because the minds of those workers were, more than the minds of most others, in sympathy with the Infinite mind. While at work their hands were more distinctly guided by the Almighty hand; they felt and embodied more of the spirit which makes, which is, life.

Here is a frame of canvas, a block of marble, a pile of stones, a vocabulary. Of the canvas you make a screen, you build a dwelling with the pile of stones, chisel a door-sill out of the block, with the vocabulary you write an essay. And in each case you work well and creatively, if your work be in harmony with God's laws, if your screen be light, sightly, and protective, your dwelling healthful and commodious, your sill lie solid and square, your essay be judicious and sound. But if on the canvas you have a Christ's head by Leonardo, out of the pile of stones a Strasburg Cathedral, from the block of marble a Venus of Milo, with the vocabulary a tragedy of Hamlet, you have works which are so creative that they tell on the mind with the vivid, impressive, instructive, never-wearying delight of the works of nature. The men who wrought them were strong to do so through the vigor of their sympathy with what Plato calls the formative principle of the universe, they thereby becoming themselves creators, that is, poets. And we sacredly guard their creations among our best treasures of human gift, because they are so spiritually alive that whenever we put ourselves in relation with them they animate us, they spiritualize our thoughts; and this they do because the minds whence they issued were radiant centers of ideal power, that is, power to conceive the beautiful.

But what is ideal power? the reader may ask. He might likewise ask, What is moral power? And unless he has in his own mind some faculty of moral estimation, no answer will help him. That which comes to us through feeling cannot be intellectually defined, can only be appreciated through feeling. By describing its effects and accompaniments we approach to a knowledge of what it is. By means of a foot-rule you can make clear to every member of a crowd what is the height of the Apollo Belvedere, and the exact length of the statue's face; and each one can for himself verify the accuracy of your statement. But not with a like distinctness and vivacity of assent can you get the crowd to go along with you as to the Apollo's beauty. Acknowledgment of the beautiful in art implies a degree of culture and a native susceptibility not to be found in every accidental gathering. Full and sincere assent to your declaration that the statue is very beautiful presupposes a high ideal in the mind; that is, a lofty pre-attained idea of what is manly beauty. But after all, the want of unanimity of assent to a moral or an æsthetic position, does it not come from the difficulty and subtlety of the idea to be pre-attained? Assent even to an intellectual proposition, does not it too presuppose an ideal in the mind of him who assents? When you show by visible measurement that the statue is eight feet high, whoever understands what you mean must have already in his head the idea of what one foot is; that is, he must carry within him an ideal. No tittle of information, not the slightest accession of knowledge, will you derive from the measurement even of the area of a hall or of the cubic contents of a block, unless you bring with you in your mind an idea, an ideal, of what is a superficial or a cubic square foot.

Attempts to give a notion of what the beautiful is, by enumerating some of the physical conditions that are found to be present in artistic figures or persons distinguished for beauty, or attempts to produce what shall be beautiful, by complying with these conditions, come no nearer to the aim than do compounded mineral waters to the briskness and flavor of a fresh draught from the original spring. In the analysis there may be no flaw; the ingredients are chemically identical in quality and proportion; but the nameless, inimitable, inscrutable life is wanting: the mixing has been done by a mechanical, not by a creative hand. Haydon says, "The curve of the circle is excess, the straight line is deficiency, the ellipsis is the degree between, and that curve, added to or united with proportion, regulates the form and features of a perfect woman." Mr. D. R. Hay, in a series of books, professes to have discovered the principles of beauty in the law of harmonic ratio, without, however, "pretending," as he modestly and wisely declares, "to give rules for that kind of beauty which genius alone can produce in high art." The discovery of Mr. Hay is curious and fascinating, and, like the announcement of Haydon, may give practical hints to artists and others. But no intellectual process or ingenuity can make up for the absence of emotional warmth and refined selection. "Beauty, the foe of excess and vacuity, blooms, like genius, in the equilibrium of all the forces," says Jean Paul. "Beauty," says Hemsterhuis, "is the product of the greatest number of ideas in the shortest time," which is like the Italian definition, *il piu nel' uno*, unity in multiplicity, believed by Coleridge to contain the principle of beauty. On another page of the "Table Talk" Coleridge is made to say, "You are wrong in resolving beauty into expression or interest; it is quite distinct; indeed, it is opposite, although not contrary. Beauty is an immediate presence, between which and the beholder *nihil est*. It is always one and tranquil; whereas the interesting always disturbs and is disturbed." Hegel, in his "Æsthetic," defines natural beauty to be "the idea as immediate unity, in so far as this unity is visible in sensuous reality." And a few pages earlier he is more brief and distinct, calling the beautiful "the sensuous shining forth of the idea." And Schelling, in his profound treatise on "The Relation of the Plastic Arts to Nature," says, "The beautiful is beyond form; it is substance, the universal; it is the look and expression of the spirit of Nature." Were it not better and more precise to say that it is to us the look and expression of the spiritual when this is peering through choicest embodiments? But we will stop with definitions. After endeavoring, by means of sentences and definitions to get a notion of the beautiful, one is tempted to say, as Goethe did when "the idea of the Divinity" was venturously mentioned to him by Eckermann, "Dear child, what know we of the idea of the Divinity? and what can our narrow ideas tell of the Highest Being? Should I, like a Turk, name it with a hundred names, I should still fall short, and, in comparison with the infinite attributes, have said nothing."

We have called the beautiful the light of the mind; but there must be mind to be illuminated. If your torch be waved in a chamber set round with bits of granite and slate and pudding-stone, you will get no luminous reverberation. But brandish it before rubies and emeralds and diamonds! The qualities in the mind must be precious, in order that the mind become radiant through beauty. To take a broad example.

The Hindoos in their organization have a fine

sense of the beautiful, but they lack mental breadth and bottom; and hence their life and literature are not strong and manifold, although in both there are exhibitions of that refinement which only comes of sensibility to the beautiful. The Chinese, on the other hand, are wanting in this sensibility; hence their prosaic, finite civilization. But most noteworthy is the contrast between them in religious development. In that of the Hindoos there was expansion, vastness, self-merging in infinitude; the Chinese are religiously contracted, petty, idolatrous; a contrast which I venture to ascribe, in large measure, to the presence in the one case, and the absence in the other, of the inspiration of the beautiful.

To the same effect individual examples might be cited innumerable. Look at Wordsworth and Byron, both preëminent for sensibility to the beautiful; but, from deep diverseness in other leading mental gifts, the one, through the light of this vivifying power, became a poet of the propensities and the understanding, a poet of passion and wit; the other, a poet of the reason, a poet of nature and meditative emotion.

To do their best the moral feelings, too, need the light and inward stimulus of the beautiful;

but if these feelings are by nature weak, no strength or intensity of the sense of beauty will have power to get from a mind thus deficient high moral thought or action. If there be present the accomplishment of verse, we shall have a Byron; or, the other poetic gifts in full measure, with lack of this accomplishment, and we may get a Beckford, who builds Fonthill Abbeys, and with purity and richness of diction describes palaces, actual or feigned, and natural scenery with picturesqueness and genial glow; or, the intellectual endowments being mediocre, we shall have merely a man of superficial taste; or, the moral regents being ineffective, an intellectual sybarite, or a refined voluptuary. Like the sun, the beautiful shines on healthful field and poisonous fen; and her warmth will even make flowers to bloom in the fen, but it is not in her to make them bear refreshing odors or nourishing fruit.

As men have body, intellect, and moral natures, so is there physical, intellectual, and spiritual beauty, and each distinct from the others. Take first a few examples from the domain of art. The body and limbs of the Gladiator in the Louvre may be cited as the exponent of corporeal beauty; the face of the Apollo Belvedere as that of intellectual and physical; and the Santo Sisto Madonna of Raphael, and the Christ of the Last Supper by Leonardo da Vinci, for spiritual. Through these radiant creations we look into the transcendent minds of their artists with a chastened, exalting joy, not unmingled with pride in our brotherhood with such beauty-lifted co-workers with God.

Among the higher races, life is affluent in examples of the three kinds of beauty, two of them, and even all three, at times united in one subject. Children and youth offer the most frequent instances of physical beauty. Napoleon's face combined in high degree both physical and intellectual, without a trace of moral beauty. Discoveries in science, and the higher scientific processes, as likewise broad and intense intellectual action, exemplify often intellectual beauty. Of moral beauty history preserves examples which are the brightest jewels, and the most precious, in the casket of mankind's memory; among the most brilliant of which are the trust of Alexander, when he drank the draught from the hand of his physician, though warned that it was poisoned; the fidelity of the paroled Regulus, returning from Rome to the enemy into the jaws of a certain and cruel death; Sir Philip Sidney, wounded unto death, taking the cup of water untasted from his parched lips, to give it to a dying soldier; Luther at the Diet of Worms; the public life of Washington; the life and death of Socrates, and especially that last act of washing his body to save the women the trouble of washing it a few hours later, when it would be a corpse; and, lastly, that most beautiful of lives and most sublime of deaths, which live in the heart of Christendom as its exemplar and ever fresh ideal.

There is no province of honorable human endeavor, no clean inlet opened by the senses or the intellect or the feelings, into which from that vast, deep, oceanic spring, the human soul, the beautiful does not send its fructifying tides. There is no height in history but is illuminated by its gleam. Only through the beautiful can truth attain its full stature; only through the beautiful can the heart be perfectly purified; only with vision purged by the beautiful can anything be seen in its totality. All other faculties it makes prolific; it is the mental generator. It helps to unveil, and then welds, the link between the visible and the invisible. It inspires feeling (which is ever the source of deepest insight) to discover excellence; it quickens the mind to creative activity; it is forever striving upward. Without the spiritual fervor of the beautiful, your religion is narrow and superstitious, your science cramped and mortal, your life unripened. In the mind it kindles a flame that discloses the divinity there is in all things. Lightning bares to the awed vision the night-shrouded earth; more vivid than lightning, the flash of the beautiful reveals to the soul the presence of God.

II.

WHAT IS POETRY?

The better to meet the question, *What* is poetry? we begin by putting before it another, and ask, *Where* is poetry? Poetry is in the mind. Landscapes, rainbows, sunsets, constellations, these exist not to the stag, the hare, the elephant. To them nature has no aspects, no appearances modified by feeling. Furnished with neither combining intellect nor transmuting sensibility, they have no vision for aught but the proximate and immediate and the animally necessary. Corporeal life is all their life. Within the life of mind poetry is born, and in the best and deepest part of that life.

The whole world outside of man, and, added to this, the wider world of his inward motions, whether these motions interact on one another or be started and modified by what is without them, all this — that is, all human life, in its endless forms, varieties, degrees, all that can come within the scope of man — is the domain of poetry; only, to enjoy, to behold, to move about in, even to enter this domain, the individual man must bear within him a light that shall transfigure whatever it falls on, a light of such subtle quality, of such spiritual virtue, that wherever it strikes it reveals something of the very mystery of being.

In many men, in whole tribes, this light is so feebly nourished that it gives no illumination. To them the two vast worlds, the inner and the outer, are made up of opaque facts, cognizable, available, by the understanding, and by it handled grossly and directly. Things, conditions, impressions, feelings, are not taken lovingly into the mind, to be made there prolific through higher contacts. They are not dandled joyfully in the arms of the imagination. Imagination! Before proceeding a step further, — nay, in order that we be able to proceed safely, — we must make clear to ourselves what means this great word, imagination.

The simplest intellectual work is to perceive physical objects. Having perceived an object several times, the intellect lifts itself to a higher process, and knows it when it sees it again, remembers it. *Perception* is the first, the simplest, the initiatory intellectual process, *memory* is the second. Higher than they, and rising out of them, is a third process, the one whereby are modified and transmuted the mental impressions of what is perceived or remembered. A mother, just parted from her child, recalls his form and face, summons before *her mind's eye* an image of him; and this image is modified by her feelings, she seeing him in attitudes and relations in which she had never seen him before, cheerful or sad according to her mood. This she could not do by aid of memory alone; she could not vary the impress of her boy left on the brain; she could not vividly reproduce it in shifting, rapidly successive conditions; she could not modify and diversify that impress; in a word, she could not liberate it. Memory could only re-give her, with single, passive fidelity, what she had seen, unmodified, motionless, unenlivened, like a picture of her boy on canvas. Urge intellectual activity to the phase above memory, and the mental image steps out from its immobility, becomes a changeful, elastic figure, brightened or darkened by the lights and shadows cast by the feelings; the intellect, quick now with plastic power, varying the image in position and expression, obedient to the demands of the feelings, of which it is ever the ready instrument. This third process is *imagination.*

Through this mode of intellectual action the materials gathered in the mind are endlessly combined and modified. In all intellectual activity, beyond bare perception and memory, imagination in some degree is and must be present. It is in fact the mind handling its materials, and in no sphere, above the simplest, can the mind move without this power of firmly holding and molding facts and relations, phenomena and interior promptings and suggestions. To the forensic reasoner, to the practical master-worker in whatever sphere, such a power is essential not less than to the ideal artist or to the weaver of fictions. Imagination is thus the abstract action, that is, the most intense action, of the intellect.

When I run over in my mind, and in the order of their service, the first seven presidents of the United States, Washington, Adams, Jefferson, Madison, Monroe, Adams, Jackson, I exert only memory. The moment I begin to compare or contrast one with another, or to give the character of any of them, I put into play the higher, the imaginative action; for, to draw an historical character, the facts collected by memory must be shaped and colored and organized, the details gathered must be combined into a whole by the intellect, which being a mere tool, the success of the result (the tool being of a temper to do the work laid on it) will depend on the quality of the powers that handle it, that is, on the writer's gifts of sympathy.

The degree and fullness wherewith the imaginative power shall be called upon depending thus on faculties of feeling, thence it is that the word *imagination* has come to be appropriated to the highest exercise of the power, that, namely, which is accomplished by those few who, having more than usual emotive capacity in combination with sensibility to the beautiful, are hereby stimulated to mold and shape into fresh forms the stores gathered by perception and memory, or the material originated within the mind through its creative fruitfulness. In strictness, this exaltation of intellectual action should be called *poetic* imagination.

To imagine is, etymologically speaking, *with* the mind to form *in* the mind an image; that is, by inward power to produce an interior form, a something substantial made out of what we term the unsubstantial. To imagine is thus always, in a certain sense, to create; and even men of dullest mentality have this power in *kind*. The *degree* in which men have it makes one of the chief differences among them. The power is inherent, is implied in the very existence of the human mind. When it is most lively the mind creates out of all it feels and hears and sees, taking a simple sight or hint or impression or incident, and working out images, making much out of little, a world out of an atom. Akin herein to the supreme creative might, the man of highest imagination, the poet, unrolls out of his brain, through vivid energy, new worlds, peopled with thought, throbbing with humanity.

When we imagine, therefore, we hold an image in the mind, grasping it with spiritual fingers, just as by our corporeal fingers a physical substance is grasped. Now the poetic mind in handling the image tosses it with what might be called a sportive earnest delight, and through this power and freedom of *play* elicits by sympathetic fervor, from its very core, electric rays, wherein the subject glows like the sculpture on an inwardly illuminated urn; rare insights being thus vouchsafed to clearest imaginative vision, — insights gained never but through sensibilities elevated and purified by aspirations after, and gleaming glimpses of, the absolute and ideal, the intellect being used as an obedient cheerful servant.

The sensibility that is so finely strung as to have these glimpses, revels in them as its fullest happiness, and with its whole might seeks and courts them. Hence the mind thus privileged to live nearer than others to the absolutely true, the spiritual ideal, is ever plying its privilege: conceiving, heightening, spiritualizing, according to the vision vouchsafed it; through this vision beholding everywhere a better and fairer than outwardly appears; painting nature and humanity, not in colors fictitious or fanciful, but in those richer, more lucent ones which such minds, through the penetrating insight of the higher imagination, see more truly as they are than minds less creatively endowed.

Thus is imagination a power inherent in, essential to, all intellectual action that ranges above simple perception and memory; a power without which the daily business of life even could not go on, being that power whereby the mind manipulates, so to speak, its materials. In its higher phasis it may be defined as the intellect stimulated by feeling to multiply its efforts for the ends of feeling; and in its highest it may be said to be intellect winged by emotion to go forth and gather honey from the bloom of creation.

Imagination, then, being intellect in keenest chase, and the intellectual part of the mind being, when moved in concert with the effective part, but a tool of this, what are the feelings or conditions of feeling of which intellect becomes the instrument in the production of poetry?

Cast your look on a page filled with the titles of Shakespeare's plays. What worlds of throbbing life lie behind that roll! Then run over the persons of a single drama: that one bounded inclosure, how rich in variety and intensity, and truth of feeling! And when you shall have thus cursorily sent your mind through each and all, tragic, comic, historic, lyric, you will have traversed in thought, accompanied by hundreds of infinitely diversified characters, wide provinces of human sorrow and joy. Why are these pictures of passion so uniquely prized, passed on from generation to generation, the most precious heir-loom of the English tongue, to-day as fresh as on the morning when the paper was moist with the ink wherewith they were first written? Because they have in them more fullness and fineness and fidelity than any others. The poet has more life in him than other men, and Shakespeare has in him more life than any other poet, life manifested through power of intellect exalted through union with power of sympathy, the embodiments whereof are rounded, enlarged, refined, made translucent by that gift of *sensibility to the fair and perfect*[1] whereby, according to its degree, we are put in more loving relation to the work of God, and gain the clearest insights into his doings and purposes; a gift without which in richest measure Shakespeare might have been a notable historian or novelist or philosopher, but never the supreme poet he is.

When Coriolanus, having led the Volscians to Rome, encamps under its walls, and the Romans, in their peril and terror, send to him a deputation to move him from his vengeful purpose, the deputies, — the foremost citizens of Rome and the relations and former friends of Coriolanus, — having "declared their business in a very modest and humble manner," he is described by Plutarch as stern and austere, answering them with "much bitterness and high resentment of the injuries done him." What

[1] See preceding Essay.

was the temper as well as the power of Coriolanus, we learn distinctly enough from these few words of Plutarch. But the task of the poet is more than this. To our imagination, that is, to the abstracting intellect roused by sympathy to a semi-creative state, he must present the haughty Roman so as to fill us with an image of him that shall in itself embody that momentous hour in the being of the young republic. He must dilate us to the dimensions of the man and the moment; he must so enlarge and warm our feeling that it shall take in, and delight in, the grandeur of the time and the actors. The life of Rome, of Rome yet to be so mighty, is threatened by one of her own sons. This vast history, to be for future centuries that of the world, a Roman seemed about to quench, about to rase the walls that were to embrace the imperial metropolis of Europe, Asia, and Africa. Of what gigantic dimensions must he be, this Roman! Now hear Menenius, a former friend and admirer of Coriolanus, depict him. Having described, in those compressed sinewy phrases which Shakespeare has at command, the change in his nature, he adds, "When he walks, he moves like an engine, and the ground shrinks before his treading. He is able to pierce a corselet with his eye; he talks like a knell, and his hum is a battery. He sits in his state, as a thing made for Alexander. What he bids be done is finished with his bidding: he wants nothing of a god but eternity and a heaven to throne in."

Hear how a mother's heart, about to break, from the loss of her son, utters its grief when it has the privilege of using a voice quivering with poetic fervor. The French king bids Lady Constance be comforted: she answers, —

"No, I defy all counsel, all redress,
But that which ends all counsel, true redress,
Death, death. O amiable lovely death!
Thou odoriferous stench! sound rottenness!
Arise forth from the couch of lasting night,
Thou hate and terror to prosperity,
And I will kiss thy detestable bones;
And put my eyeballs in thy vaulty brows;
And ring these fingers with thy household worms;
And stop this gap of breath with fulsome dust,
And be a carrion monster like thyself:
Come, grin on me; and I will think thou smil'st:
And buss thee as thy wife! Misery's love,
O, come to me!"

In these two passages from "Coriolanus" and "King John" what magnificence of hyperbole! The imagination of the reader, swept on from image to image, is strained to follow that of the poet. And yet, to the capable, how the pile of amplification lifts out the naked truth. Read these passages to a score of well-clad auditors, taken by chance from the thoroughfare of a wealthy city, or from the benches of a popular lecture-room. To the expanded mold wherein the passages are wrought, a few — five or six, perhaps, of the twenty — would be able to fit their minds, zestfully climbing the poet's climax. To some they would be dazzling, semi-offensive extravagance, prosaic minds not liking, because seeing but dimly by, the poetically imaginative light. And to some they would be grossly unintelligible, the enjoyment of the few full appreciators seeming to them unnatural or affected.

Now, the enjoyment of the few appreciators, what is its source? By these passages certain feelings in them are made to vibrate and are pitched to a high key. A very comprehensive word is feelings. What is the nature of those feelings thus wrought upon?

The elementary feelings of our nature, when in healthful function, are capable of emitting spiritual light; and, when exalted to their purest action, do and must emit such, the inward fire sending forth clear flame unmixed with smoke. To perceive this light, and, still more, to have your path illuminated thereby, implies the present activity of some of the higher human sensibilities ; and to be so organized as to be able to embody in words, after having imagined, personages, conditions, and conjunctions whence this light shall flash on and ignite the sensibilities of others, implies, besides vivid sympathies and delight in the beautiful, a susceptibility to the manifestations of moral and intellectual life which is enjoyed only by him in whom the nobler elements of being are present in such intensity, proportions, and quality, and are so commingled, that he can reproduce life itself with translucent truthfulness, he becoming, through this exalting susceptibility, poet or maker.

What constitutes the wealth of human life? Is it not fullness and richness of feeling? To refine this fullness, to purify this richness, to distill the essence out of this wealth, to educate the feelings by revealing their subtle possibilities, by bringing to light the divinity there is within and behind them, this is the poet's part ; and this, his great part, he can only do by being blest with more than common sympathy with the spirit of the Almighty Creator, and thence clearer insight into his work and will. Merely to embody in verse the feelings, thoughts, deeds, scenes of human life, is not the poet's office; but to exhibit these as having attained, or as capable of attaining, the power and beauty and spirituality possible to each. The glorifier of humanity the poet is, not its mere reporter; that is the historian's function. The poet's business is not with facts as such, or with inferences, but with truth of feeling, and the very spirit of truth. His function is ideal; that is, from the prosaic, the individual, the limited, he is to lift us up to the universal, the generic, the boundless. In compassing this noble end he may, if such be his bent, use the facts and feelings and individualities of daily life; and, by illuminating and ennobling them he will approve his human insight, as well as his poetic gift.

The generic in sentiment, the universal, the infinite, can only be reached and recognized through the higher feelings, through those whose activity causes emotion. The simple impulses, the elementary loves, are in themselves bounded in their action near and direct; but growing round the very fountain of life, having their roots in the core of being, they are liable to strike beyond their individual limits, and this they do with power when under their sway the whole being is roused and expanded. When by their movement the better nature is urged to heroism and self-sacrifice, as in the story of Damon and Pythias, the reader or beholder is lifted into the atmosphere of finest emotion ;· for then the impulse has reached its acme of function, and playing in the noonday of the beautiful, the contemplation of it purges and dilates us. We are upraised to the disinterested mood, the poetical, in which mood there is ever imaginative activity refined by spiritual necessities. It is not extravagant to affirm that when act or thought reaches the beautiful, it resounds through the whole being, tuning it like a high strain of sweetest music. Thus in the poetical (and there is no poetry until the sphere of the beautiful is entered) there is always a reverberation from the emotional nature. Reverberation implies space, an ample vault of roof or of heaven. In a tight, small chamber there can be none. If feeling is shut within itself, there is no reëcho. Its explosion must rebound from the roomy dome of sentiment, in order that it become musical.

The moment you enter the circle of the beautiful, into which you can only be ushered by a light within yourself, a light kindled through livelier recognition of the divine spirit, — the moment you draw breath in this circle you find yourself enlarged, spiritualized, buoyed above the self. No matter how surrounded, or implicated, or enthralled, while you are there, be it but for a few moments, you are liberated.

"No more — no more — oh! never more on me
The freshness of the heart can fall like dew,
Which out of all the lovely things we see
Extracts emotions beautiful and new,
Hived in our bosoms like the bag o' the bee.
Think'st thou the honey with those objects grew?
Alas! 't was not in them, but in thy power
To double even the sweetness of a flower."

"All who joy would win
Must share it; happiness was born a twin."

"He entered in the house, — his home no more,
For without hearts there is no home — and felt
The solitude of passing his own door
Without a welcome; *there* he long had dwelt,
There his few peaceful days Time had swept o'er,
There his worn bosom and keen eye would melt
Over the innocence of that sweet child,
His only shrine of feelings undefiled."

These three passages are from a poem in which there is more wit than poetry, and more cynicism than either; a poem in spirit unsanctified, Mephistophelian, written by a man of the world, a terrible egotist, *blasé* already in early manhood, in whose life, through organization, inherited temperament, and miseducation, humanity was so cramped, distorted, envenomed, that the best of it was in the fiery sway of the more urgent passions, his inmost life being, as it must always be with poets, inwoven into his verse. From the expiring volcano in his bosom his genius, in this poem, casts upon the world a lurid flame, making life look pale or fever-flushed. With unslumbering vivacity, human nature is exhibited in that misleading light made by the bursting of half-truths that relate to its lower side, a light the more deceptious from the sparkling accompaniment of satire and wit.

Above the pungent secularities, the nimble intellectualities, the specious animalism, the derisive skepticism, the snapping personalities, the witty worldliness, that interlace and constitute the successive cantos of "Don Juan," the passages just quoted and similar ones (they are not many) rise, as above the desires and the discontents, the plots and contentions, the shrewd self-seekings of a heated, noisy city rises a Gothic spire, aspiring, beautiful, drawing most of its beauty from its aspiration, on whose pinnacle, calmly glistening in the upper air, plays the coming and the parting day, while shadows fill the streets below, and whose beauty throws over the town a halo that beckons men from afar. The spire, in its steadfast tranquillity and its beauty, so unlike the restless wrangling dissonance below it, grew nevertheless out of the same hearts that make the dissonance, and, typifying what is spiritual and eternal in them, tends by its ideal presence to enlarge and uplift those by whose eyes it is sought. These upshootings in "Don Juan" irradiate the cantos, giving an attractiveness which draws to them eyes that otherwise would not have known them; and if too pure in their light and too remote to mingle directly with the flare and flash that dazzle without illuminating, silently they shine and steadily, an unconscious heavenly influence, above these coruscations of earthly thoughts, — thoughts telling from their lively numerousness, but neither grand nor deep.

From the same solar center fall frequently single rays that make lines and stanzas glisten, and but for which this poem, lacking their perfusive light, would soon pass into oblivion; for from the beautiful it is that the satire, the wit, the voluptuousness get their sparkle and their sheen. If passages morally censurable are hereby made more captivating, we are not content with saying that God's sun fructifies and beautifies poison-oak and hemlock; but we affirm that the beautiful, being by its nature necessarily pure, communicates of its quality to whoever becomes aware of it, and thus in some measure counterweighs the lowering tendency. Moreover, the morally bad, deriving its character of evil from incompleteness, from the arresting or the perversion of good, like fruit plucked unripe, and being therefore outside the pale of the beautiful (the nature of which is completeness, fullness, perfection of life) cannot by itself be made captivating through the beautiful. Iago and Edmund are poetical as parts of a whole; and when in speech they approach the upper region of thought, it is because the details allotted to them have to be highly wrought for the sake of the general plot and effect, and further, because humanity and truth speak at times through strange organs. Besides, the ideal may be used to show more glaringly the hideousness of evil, and thence Iago and Edmund, as ideal villains, through the very darkness in which only poetic art could have enveloped them, help us by indirection to see and value the lights that surround the noble and the good.

In healthy function all the feelings are pure and moral, those whose action is most earthly and animal and selfish uniting themselves at their highest with the spiritual, for performance whose compass reaches beyond an individual, momentary good. A burglar or a murderer may exhibit courage; but here, a manly quality backing baseness and brutality for selfish, short-sighted ends, there is an introverted and bounded action, no expansive upward tendency, and thence no poetry. But courage, when it is the servant of principle for large, unselfish ends, becomes poetical, exhibiting the moral beautiful, as in the fable of Curtius and the fact (or fable) of Winkelried. In the poetical there is always enlargement, exaltation, purification; animal feeling, self-seeking propensity, becoming so combined with the higher nature as to rise above themselves, above the self.

The lioness, pursuing the robber of her cub, if in her rage she scarcely heed that he (to stay her steps) has dropped the cub in her path, but, casting at it a glance of recognition, bounds with a wilder howl after the robber, the incident is purely bestial, an exhibition of sheer brute fury, and as such repulsive and most unpoetical. But let her, instantly drawing her fiery eye from the robber, stop, and for the infuriated roar utter a growl of leonine tenderness over her recovered cub, and our sympathy leaps towards her. Through the red glare of rage there shines suddenly a stream of white light, gushing from one of the purest fountains: wrathful fury is suddenly subdued by love. A moment before she was possessed with savage fierceness, her blood boiling with hate and revenge; now it glows with a mother's joy. Her nature rises to the highest whereof it is capable. It is the poetry of animalism.

In the poetical, thought is amplified and ripened, while purified, in the calm warmth of emotion. From being emotive, poetry draws in more of the man, and higher, finer powers, than prose. The poetical has, must have, rotundity. No poet ever had a square head. Prose, in its naked quality, is to poetry what a skeleton is to a moving, flesh-and-spirit-endowed body. From the skeleton you can learn osteology, but neither æsthetics nor human nature. Imaginative prose partakes of the spiritual character of poetry. When a page is changed from poetry into prose it is flattened, deadened; when from prose into poetry it is uplifted, enlivened. You get a something else and a something more. Reduced to plain prose, the famous passage from the mouth of Viola in "Twelfth Night" would read somewhat thus: "My father had a daughter who loved a man and would let no one know of her love, but concealed it, until her cheek grew pale with grief, patiently bearing within her bosom the misery of an untold attachment." Now hear the poet: —

> "She never told her love,
> But let concealment, like a worm i' the bud,
> Feed on her damask cheek: she pined in thought:
> And with a green and yellow melancholy
> She sat like patience on a monument,
> Smiling at grief."

What has been done with the prose statement? Instead of a bare fact we have a picture, a twofold picture; and this, in its compact, fresh, rose-tinted vividness, carries the whole into our hearts with a tenfold success. Through emotional joy we apprehend, as by the light of an instantaneous ignition, the state of the sufferer. The prose-report is a smoldering fire on the hearth, through whose sleepy smoke there comes a partial heat; the poetic is the flame in full fervor, springing upward, illuminating, warming the heart, delighting the intellect. The imagination of the reader, quickened by illustrations so apt and original, is by their beauty tuned to its most melodious key, while by the rare play of intellectual vitality his mind is dilated. He has become mentally a richer man, enriched through the refining and enlarging of his higher sensibilities, and the activity imparted to his intellect.

To say of a man that he is without imagination were to say he is an idiot; that is, one lacking the inward force and the inward instruments to grasp and handle the materials collected from without by perception and memory, and from within by consciousness. To say of a poet that he is without poetic imagination were to say he is no poet. What is poetic imagination? This, for our theme, is a vital question. Can there be given to it an approximate answer?

Figure to yourself a company of men and women in presence of a September sunset near the sea, the eye taking in at once ocean and a variegated landscape. The company must not be a score of tawny American aborigines, nor of European peasants, nor of individuals whose life of monotonous labor, whether for necessaries or luxuries, has no opportunity or no will for the finer mental culture; but, to give aptness to our illustration, should consist of persons whose being has been unfolded to the tissue of susceptibility to the wonders and beauties of nature, and whose intellect has been tilled sufficiently to receive and nourish any fresh seed of thought that may be thrown upon it; in short, a score of cultivated adults. The impression made by such a scene on such a company is heightened by a rare atmospheric calm. The heart of each gazer fills with emotion, at first unutterable except by indefinite exclamation; when one of the company says, —

> "A fairer face of evening cannot be."

These words, making a smooth iambic line, give some utterance, and therefore some relief, to the feeling of all. Then another adds, —

> "The holy time is quiet as a nun
> Breathless with adoration."

Instantly the whole scene, steeped in the beams of the sinking sun, is flooded with a light that illuminates the sunlight, a spiritual light. The scene is transfigured before their eyes: it is as if the heavens had opened, and inundated all its features with a celestial subtilizing aura. How has this been accomplished? The first line has little of the quality of poetic imagination.

"A fairer face of evening cannot be."

is simple and appropriate, but in it there is no fresh glow, no mysterious throb. Above the level of this line rise suddenly the first three words of the second, "the holy time." The presence of a scene where sky, earth, and ocean combine for the delight of the beholders puts them in a mood which crowns the landscape with a religious halo. That the time is holy they all feel; and now, to make its tranquillity appreciable by filling the heart with it, the poet adds — "is quiet as a nun breathless with adoration." By this master-stroke of poetic power the atmospheric earthly calm is vivified with, is changed into, super-earthly calm. By a fresh burst of spiritual light the mind is set æsthetically aglow, as by the beams of the setting sun the landscape is physically. By an exceptionally empowered hand the soul is strung to a high key. Fullness and range of sensibility open to the poet [1] a wide field of illustration; its exacting fineness reveals the

[1] Wordsworth.

one that carries his thought into the depths of the reader's mind, bringing him that exquisite joy caused by keen intellectual power in the service of pure emotion.

Take now other samples from the treasury of choicest poetry. Here is one from Coleridge: —

> "And winter, slumbering in the open air,
> Wears on his smiling face a dream of spring."

Here again the intellect is urged to its highest action, the abstract or imaginative action, to do the hests of a sensibility so finely wrought by the inward impulsion to seek for the most exquisite that nature can furnish, that it yields similitudes most delicate, most apt, most expressive.

Milton thus opens the fifth book of "Paradise Lost:" —

> "Now morn, her rosy steps in the eastern clime
> Advancing, sowed the earth with orient pearl."

Shakespeare makes Romeo describe daybreak: —

> "And jocund day
> Stands tiptoe on the misty mountain-tops."

Keats begins "Hyperion" with these lines:

> "Deep in the shady sadness of a vale,
> Far sunken from the healthy breath of morn."

In the Monody on Keats, Shelley, describing

the lamentation of nature at his death, concludes a stanza as follows:—

"Morning sought
Her eastern watch-tower, and, her hair unbound,
Wet with the tears that should adorn the ground,
Dimmed the aerial eyes that kindle day;
Afar the melancholy thunder moaned,
Pale Ocean in unquiet slumber lay,
And the wild winds flew around, sobbing in their dismay."

Such passages are the very flower of poetry, thought exquisitely dyed in sentiment, laying suddenly bare a picture with so much light in it that each passage irradiates its page and the reader's mind. By their happiness the similitudes emphasize and enforce the thought; and they do a higher service than this; for, being a breath from the inner life of genius, they blow power into the reader. To translate these passages into prose were like trying to translate a lily into the mold out of which it springs, or a bar of Beethoven into the sounds of the forum, or the sparkle of stars into the warmth of a coal fire.

The best poetry has a far background; it comes out of deeps within the poet, unfathomed by himself, unfathomable. He feels more than he can express. Hence the imaginative poet always suggests, revealing enough to inspirit the reader's higher faculties to strive for more; not because, with artistic design, he leaves much untold, which he often does, but because through imaginative susceptibility he at times grasps at and partly apprehends much that cannot be embodied. He feels his subject more largely and deeply than he can see or represent it. To you his work is suggestive because to him the subject suggested more than he could give utterance to. Every subject, especially every subject of poetic capability, having infinite relations, he who most apprehends this boundlessness — and indeed because he does apprehend it — can do or say what will open it to you or me; and the degree of his genius is measured by the extent to which he can present or expose it. The unimaginative gives surface-work, and, suggesting nothing, is at once exhausted.

The poetic imagination shows itself in the epithets the poet has at his command, creative insight drawing an epithet out of the heart of an object; whence, there is beneath such an epithet a depth that keeps feeding it with significance, bringing out its aptness the longer we look. Sometimes epithets are brighter than their object; the unimaginative thus futilely striving to impart power instead of deriving it. To be lasting, the light of the epithet must be struck by the imagination out of its object. The inspired poet finds a word so sympathetic with the thought that it caresses and hugs it.

Depth and breadth of nature are implied in the full poetic imagination. The love of the beautiful, wielding a keen intellect, needs furthermore rich material to mold, and only out of the poet's individual resources can this be drawn. To make a high artist, you must have very much of a man. Behind "Paradise Lost" and "Samson Agonistes" is a big Miltonic man. The poet has to put a great deal of himself, and the best of him, into his work; thence, for high poetry, there must be a great deal of high self to put in. He must coin his soul, and have a large soul to coin; the best work cannot be made out of materials gathered by memory and fancy. His stream of thought must flow from springs, not from reservoirs. Hence the universal biographical interest in such men; they have necessarily a rich personality.

The passages I have cited are all pictures of outward nature, natural scenes mirrored on the mind, or rather refracted through it, and in the act transfigured, spiritualized; for such scenes, having the fortune to fall on the minds of poets, are reproduced with joyful revelation of their inmost being, as sunbeams are through a crystal prism. Exhibiting material nature spiritualized, well do these passages show the uplifting character of poetic imagination. But this displays a higher, and its highest power when, striking like a thunderbolt into the core of things, it lays bare mysteries of God and of the heart which mere prosaic reason cannot solve or approach, cannot indeed alone even dimly apprehend.

I will now quote passages, brief ones, wherein through the poet are opened vast vistas into the shining universe, or is concentrated in single or few lines the life of man's finer nature, as in the diamond are condensed the warmth and splendor that lie latent in acres of fossil carbon.

When, in the sixth book of "Paradise Lost," Milton narrates the arrival on the battle-field of the Son, —

> "Attended by ten thousand thousand saints,"

and then adds: —

> "Far off his coming shone,"

in these five short words is a sudden glare of grandeur that dilates the capable mind with light, and, as the sublime always does, with awe.

When Ferdinand, in "The Tempest," leaps "with hair up-staring" into the sea, crying, —

"Hell is empty,
And all the devils are here,"

the mind is suddenly filled with an image of the tumult and flaming rage of a thunder-storm at sea, such as words have never elsewhere carried. What a reach in the imaginative stroke!

In the first scene of "Faust," the earth-spirit, whom Faust has evoked, concludes the whirling, dazzling, brief, but gigantic sketch of his function with these words, the majesty of which translation cannot entirely subdue: —

"I ply the resounding great loom of old Time,
And work at the Godhead's live vesture sublime."

How ennobling is the idea the mind harbors of humanity, after taking in these lines from Wordsworth's "Ode on Intimations of Immortality:" —

"But trailing clouds of glory do we come
From God, who is our home."

With a single epithet, coined for the occasion, Keats flashes upon our imagination the dethroned Saturn and the immensity of his fall:

"Upon the sodden ground
His old right hand lay nerveless, listless, dead,
Unsceptered; and his *realmless* eyes were closed."

The "Hyperion" of this transcendent genius, written in his twenty-fourth year, the year before he died, is as great poetry as has ever been treasured in words. In it he lavishes poetic wealth as though gold were with him as plenty as silver; and so on the next page he exceeds, if possible, the sublimity of the above lines, making Thea write in the catalogue of Saturn's colossal deprivations, —

> "And all the air
> Is emptied of thine hoary majesty."

These passages vividly exemplify poetic imagination, which is the illumining of a capable material by a spiritual light, a light thrown into it from the glow kindled in the poet's mind with richest sensibilities, that are refined and sublimated by an exacting, subtle inward demand for the best they can render. A single flash of new thrilling light irradiates a continent of thought. This is the work of genius, and genius is ever marked by a deeper sympathy with and recognition of the creative spirit and the divine action, a sympathy and recognition so sensitive that the spirit and action of the writer are permeated by the divine effluence, he becoming thereby the interpreter of divine law, the exhibitor of divine beauty.

In these passages the thought of the poet is thrust up through the overlaying crust of the common, by a warming, expanding, inward motion, which is sped by a vitality so urgent and irresistible that, to make passage for the new thought, lightly is lifted a load which, but for this spiritual efficacy, could not be stirred, just as heavy stones are raised by delicate growing plants. To exert this power the poet is always moved at the instance of feeling. Poetry having its birth in feeling, no man can enjoy or value it but through feeling. But what moves him to embody and shape his feeling is that ravishing sentiment which will have the best there is in the feeling, the sentiment which seeks satisfaction through contemplation or entertainment of the most divine and most perfect, and ever rises to the top of the refined joy which such contemplation educes.

The poetic imagination is the Ariel of the poet, — his spiritual messenger and Mercury. A clear look into the above passages would show that the source of their power is in the farther scope or exquisite range the imagination opens to us, often by a word. For further illustration I will take a few other examples, scrutinizing them more minutely. Had Lorenzo opened the famous passage in "The Merchant of Venice" thus, —

> "How *calm* the moonlight *lies* upon this bank,"

and continued to the end of the dozen lines in the same key, saying, —

> "There 's not the *tiniest star* that *can be seen*
> But in its *revolution* it doth *hum*,
> Aye *chanting* to the *heavenly* cherubins,"

his words would not have become celebrated and quotable. But Lorenzo has the privilege of being one of the mouth-pieces of Shakespeare, and so he begins, —

> "How *sweet* the moonlight *sleeps* upon this bank."

Two words, *sweet* and *sleep*, put in the place of *calm* and *lies*, lift the line out of prose into poetry. A log *lies* on a bank; so does a dead dog, and the more dead a thing is the more it lies; but only what is alive *sleeps*, and thus the word, besides an image of extreme stillness, brings with it what strengthens the image, the idea of change from liveliness to quiet; for that which was awake now sleeps; and the more full the picture of stillness, the more awake is the mind of the reader, awakened by the fitness and felicity of the image. The substitution of *sweet* for *calm* is, in a less degree, similarly enlivening; for, used in such conjunction, *sweet* is more individual and subtle, and imports more life, and thus helps the distinctness and vividness of the picture. How does the poetic Lorenzo word the other three lines?

> "There 's not the *smallest orb* which *thou behold'st,*
> But in *his motion like an angel sings,*
> Still *quiring* to the *young-eyed* cherubins."

The words or phrases italicized carry a larger, or a deeper or a finer meaning than the corresponding ones in the substituted lines. To *behold* is more than to *see:* it is to see contemplatively. The figure *prosopopœia* is often but an impotent straining to impart poetic life; but the personification in *in his motion* is apt and effective. *Quiring* is an amplification of the immediately preceding *sings,* and, signifying to sing in company with others, enlarges, while making more specific, the thought. And what an image of the freshness of heaven and of youthful immortality is conveyed by the epithet *young-eyed!* At every step the thought is expanded and beautiful, reaching at the end of the third line a climax on which the poetically excited mind is left poised in delight.

But the passage transformed, and, as we might say, degraded, is still poetical. There is so much poetry in the thought that the flattening of the phraseology cannot smother it, the lines still remaining poetically alive, their poetry shining through the plainer and less figurative words. And the thought is poetical because it is the result of a flight of intellect made by aid of imagination's wings, these being moved by the soaring demands of the beautiful, and beating an atmosphere exhaled from sensibility. As Joubert says, — herein uttering a cardinal æsthetic principle, — "It is, above all, in the spirituality of ideas that poetry consists." Thought that is poetic will glisten through the plainest words; whereas, if the thought be prosaic or trite, all the gilded epithets in the dictionary will not give it the poetic sheen. Perdita wishes for

> "Daffodils
> That come before the swallow dares, and take
> The winds of March with beauty."

Note the poetic potency in the simple word *dares;* how much it carries: the cold which the swallow has not the courage to confront; a mental action, I might almost call it, in the swallow, who, after making a recognizance of the season, determines that it would be rash to venture so far north: all this is in the single word. For *dares* write *does*, and the effect would be like that of cutting a gash in a rising balloon : you would let the line suddenly down, because you take the life out of the thought.

> "And take
> The winds of March with beauty."

Every one is taken at some time or other with the beauty of person or thing, and the thought is common; but that the winds of March be taken with the beauty of daffodils, this was a delicate secret which those winds would confide only to one so sympathetic as Shakespeare. This is poetic imagination, the intellect sent on far errands by a sensibility which is at once generous and bold, and fastidious through the promptings and the exactions of the beautiful.

In the opening of "Il Penseroso" Milton describes the shapes that in sprightly moods possess the fancy,

> "As thick and numberless
> As the gay motes that *people* the sunbeams."

Put *shine in* the sunbeams, for *people*, and, notwithstanding the luminousness of the word substituted, you take the sparkle out of the line, which sparkle is imparted by mental activity, and the poetic dash that has the delightful audacity to personify such atomies.

The poetical is the flush on the face of things in the unconscious triumph of their purest life, cognizable by being beheld at the moment when the higher faculties are at their fullest flood, buoyed up on the joy of being and emotional sympathy. The most and the highest of this joy is possessed by him whose imagination is most capable of being poetically agitated; for by such agitation light is engendered within him, whereby objects and sensations that before were dim and opaque grow luminous and pellucid, like great statuary in twilight or moonlight, standing vague and unvalued until a torch is waved over it.

When we begin to speak of poetry, the higher qualities of the mind come up for judgment. No genuine poet is without one or more of these, and a great poet must have most of them. Thence the thought of the poet is pitched on a high key, and even in poets of power the poetry of a page is sometimes shown merely by the sustained tone of the sentiment, giving out no jets of fire, having no passages salient with golden embossings. Through sympathy and sense of beauty, the poet gets nearer to the absolute nature of things; and thence, with little of imagery, or coloring, or passion, through this holy influence he becomes poetic, depicting by re-creating the object or feeling or condition, and rising naturally into rhythmic lines and sentences, the best substance asking for, and readily obtaining, the most suitable form of words. Yet a poet of inward resources can seldom write a page without there being heard a note or bar or passage of the finer melody.

But men wanting this inward wealth, that is, wanting depth and breadth of emotional capacity, have not, whatever their other gifts, the soil needed for highly imaginative poetry. With broad emphasis this æsthetic law is exemplified in the verse of Voltaire, especially in his dramas, and in the verse of one who was deeper and higher than he as thinker and critic, of Lessing. Skillful versifiers, by help of fancy and a certain plastic aptitude and laborious culture, are enabled to give to smooth verse a flavor of poetry and to achieve a temporary reputation. But of such uninspired workmanship the gilding after a while wears off, the externally imparted perfume surely evaporates.

Often the most suitable form of words is made of plainest, commonest parts of speech, and the fewest of them. The more intense and deep the feeling, the greater is the need of briefest, simplest utterance. When in one of those pauses of frantic wrath, — like the sudden rifts that momentarily let the calm stars through a whirling canopy of storm, — Lear utters imploringly that appeal to Heaven, the words are the familiar words of hourly use; but what divine tenderness and what sweep of power in three lines!

> "O heavens,
> If you do love old men, if your sweet sway
> Allow obedience, if yourselves are old,
> Make it your cause; send down and take my part!"

The thirty-third canto of the "Inferno" supremely exemplifies the sustaining energy of poetic imagination, that by its sublimating light it can forever hold before the mind, in tearful, irresistible beauty, one of the most woful forms of human suffering, death by starvation. In that terrific picture, in front of which all the generations of men that come after Dante are to weep purifying tears, the most exquisite stroke is given in five monosyllables; but in those five little words what depth of pathos, what concentration of meaning! On the fourth day one of Ugolino's dying sons throws himself at his father's feet, crying, —

> "Father, why dost not help me?"

Here let me remark that it is not by witnessing, through poetically imaginative representation, scenes of suffering and agony, as in this case and the tragic drama, that the sensibilities are "purged," according to the famous saying of Aristotle; but it is because such scenes are witnessed by the light of the beautiful. The beautiful always purifies and exalts.

In either of these two passages any piling up of words, any hyperbole of phrase, or boldness or even grandeur of figurative speech, would have proved a hindrance instead of a conductor to the feeling, smothering and not facilitating expression. But when, turned out of doors in "a wild night," by those "unnatural hags," his daughters, Lear, baring his brow to the storm, invokes the thunder to

"Strike flat the thick rotundity o' the world,"

there is no tenderness, no folding of the sore heart upon itself; there is the expansion of defiance, outburst of the mighty wrath of an outraged father and wronged and crownless king: and so we have a gush of the grandest diction, of the most tempestuous rhythm, the storm in Lear's mind marrying itself with a ghastly joy to the storm of the elements, the sublime tumult above echoed in the crashing splendor of the verse: —

"Blow, winds, and crack your cheeks! Rage, blow!
You cataracts and hurricanoes, spout
Till you have drenched our steeples, drowned the cocks!
You sulphurous and thought-executing fires,
Vaunt-couriers to oak-cleaving-thunderbolts,
Singe my white head! And thou, all-shaking thunder,
Strike flat the thick rotundity o' the world!
Crack nature's moulds, all germins spill at once,
That make ingrateful man!"

I know of no other single passage that exhibits so clearly the colossal dimensions of Shakespeare. Here is attained, with almost unique effect, what according to Schiller is the aim of poetry, "no other than to give to humanity its fullest possible expression, its most complete utterance."

The best poetry, like the best music, soars towards the upper light. The genuinely poetical always lifts up the thought on the swell of emotion. The thought moves free and strong because there is a deep, bubbling head of feeling behind it. Feeling, at its best, has an ascending movement, reaching up towards that high sphere where, through their conjunction, the earthly and the spiritual play in freedom in the sunshine of the beautiful. The surest test of the presence of poetry is buoyancy, springiness, which comes from the union, the divine union, of the spiritual and the beautiful. However weighty it may be with thought, the poetical passage floats, thus giving certain sign of life, of a soul irrepressible.

But as in the forest there cannot be height of stem without strength and breadth of root, the highest poetry is the most solid, the firmest set in reality, in truth. The higher a poet is, the closer hold he has of the roots of his subject. He looks at it with a peering, deeply sympathetic insight. The roots, in fact, are in himself; they are in the depths of his soul. Hence a cardinal question about a poem is, How much of it does the poet draw out of himself? Is it his by projection from his inward resources, by injection with his own juices; or is it his only by adoption and adaptation, by dress and adjustment?

Flight of poetic imagination there cannot be unless the wings have been feathered in the heart. Loftiness or grandeur of imagination there cannot be, except there be first innate richness and breadth of feeling. Imagination being simply the tensest action of intellect, is ever, like intellect in all its phases, an instrument of feeling, a mere tool. Height implies inward depth. The gift to touch the vitals of a subject is the test-gift of literary faculty; it is the soul-gift, the gift of fuller, livelier sympathy. Compare Wordsworth with Southey to learn the difference between inward and outward gifts.

Poetry being in the mind, the man who has little poetry within him will find little in nature or in the world or in Shakespeare. The man who has no music in his soul will hear none at the Conservatoire in Paris. Wordsworth sees with the inward eye, Southey too exclusively with the outward. The true poet projects visions and rhythms out from his brain, and gazes at and hearkens to them. The degree of the truthfulness to nature and the vividness of these projections is the measure of his poetic genius and capacity. Only through this intense inwardness can he attain to great visions and rhythmic raptures, and make you see and hear them. What illimitable inward sight must Keats have dwelt in ere, to depict the effect on him of looking into Chapman's Homer, he could write, —

> "Then felt I like some watcher of the skies,
> When a new planet swims into his ken;
> Or like stout Cortez, when with eagle eyes
> He stared at the Pacific, and all his men
> Looked at each other with a wild surmise,
> Silent, upon a peak in Darien."

Here is a brilliant example of poetic imagination, the intellect urged to its finest action to satisfy the feeling which delights in the grand, the select, the beautiful.

> "Silent, upon a peak in Darien."

What an outlook! What a solemn, mysterious, elevating inward moment it creates in us! To ascend to that peak, to carry the reader thither with him, that is the flight of a great poet, of one who has been — as in that choice poem, "The Prelude," Wordsworth, with an electric stroke of poetic imagination, says of Newton —

> "Voyaging through strange seas of thought, alone."

This vigor of flight in the poet, bearing on his wing the reader, whom he ushers to new, sudden vistas, is a test of poetic genius. Some poets never carry you to heights, but rather make you feel while reading them as if you were moving through shut-in valleys: their verse wants sky. They are not poetically imaginative, are not strung for those leaps which the great poet at times finds it impossible not to make. They have more poetic fancy than poetic imagination. Poetic fancy is a thin flame kindled deliberately with gathered materials;

poetic imagination is an intense flash born unexpectedly of internal collisions. Fancy is superficial and comparatively short-sighted; imagination is penetrative and far-sighted, bringing together things widely sundered, apparently diverse and opposite. Fancy divides, individualizes; imagination compounds, builds, globes. Fancy is not so broad or so keen or so warm or so bounding as imagination; is comparatively tame and cold and quiet. Imagination is synthetical. Large exhibitions of poetic imagination are rare even in the greatest poets. At its best it strikes deep into the nature of things, has a celestial quality which invests it with awe. Spenser shows great resources of fancy, but little imagination. The arc of imagination is in him too near its center. Hence there is no reach in his thoughts. He has no exhaustless depths within. He is not, as Coleridge says Shakespeare is, an example of "endless self-reproduction." Cowley, says the same great critic, "is a fanciful writer, Milton an imaginative poet."

As I have already said, the power of imagining, of forming in the mind images, conceptions, is a purely intellectual power, and imagination becomes poetical only when this intellectual power is an agent obeying that emotional power which ardently seeks, intensely longs for, the better, the more perfect, the purer, in one word, the beautiful in each province of multiform life. The willing agent, intellect, is sent out on excursions of discovery, and unexpectedly falls in with and captures all kinds of sparkling booty.

Writers weak in poetic imagination are not visited by those beaming thoughts that come unsummoned out of the invisible, like new stars which, out of the unfathomable deeps of the sky, dart suddenly upon the vision of the heaven-watcher. Such writers deal with the known, with the best commonplace, not the common merely; and under the glance of genius the common grows strange and profound.

Some poets, not weak in poetic imagination, yet use it chiefly for secondary purposes, that is, for beautifying the dress, the externals of poetry. Minds with some breadth but with little depth are not thoroughly original. Their sense of the beautiful busies itself necessarily with that for which they have the readiest gifts; and their readiest gifts being words more than ideas, versification more than thought, form more than substance, they turn out verse, chiefly narrative, which captivates through its easy flow, its smooth sensuousness of diction, its gloss. Take a poet so celebrated, in some respects so admirable, as Tennyson. Tennyson's verse is apt to be too richly dressed, too perfumed. The clothing is costlier than the thoughts can pay for. Hence at every re-reading of him he parts with some of his strength, so that after three or four repetitions he has little left for you. From a similar cause this is the case too with Byron, through whose pen to common sentiment and opinion a glow is imparted by the animal heat of the man, heightened by poetic tints from a keen sense of the beautiful. But this is not the case with Keats or Shelley or Coleridge or Wordsworth, and of course therefore not with Milton or Shakespeare. All these keep fresh, at every contact giving you strength and losing none. As freely and freshly as the sun's beams through a transparent, upspringing Gothic spire, intellect and feeling play, ever undimmed, through Shelley's "Sky-Lark." Not so through Tennyson's "Dream of Fair Women." After a time these mellifluous stanzas droop, and cling to the paper: they have not enough flame-like motion.

The nicest word-choosing will not supply the place of choice in thought, a choice prompted by fresh feeling; nor, where there is no new impulse from the heart, will the most gorgeous diction give to a line the poetic carnation. There can be no freshness of expression without freshness of thought; the sparkle on the skin comes from new blood in the heart.

Tennyson's poetry has often too much leaf and spray for the branches, and too much branch for the trunk, and too much trunk for the roots. There is not living stock enough of thought deeply set in emotion to keep the leaves ever fresh and fragrant. Wordsworth's poetry has for the most part roots deeply hidden.

Poetry is at times fitted to a subject too much like clothes to a body. This is the method with even some writers of good gifts and deserved name. Compared with Goethe, who, sensuous as he is, but healthily sensuous, writes always from within outward, Schiller is chargeable with this kind of externality. To try to make the fancy do the work of feeling is a vain effort. And so much verse is of the memory and fancy more than of the heart and imagination. Inward impulse not being dominant, the words, however shiny, are touched with coldness. Under the inward dominance (supposing always that the intellectual tool be of due temper and sharpness) the poet mounts springily on a ladder self-wrought out of the brain as he ascends ; and thus there is a prompt continuity and progressiveness, a forward and upward movement towards the climax which ever awaits you in a subject that has a poem in it. In a genuine poem, a work of inspiration and not mainly of art, there is brisk evolution, phase of feeling climbing over phase, thought kindled by thought seizing unexpected links of association. This gives sure note of the presence of the matrix out of which poetry molds itself, that is, sensibility warm and deep, penetrating sympathy. Where evolution and upward movement are not, it is a sign that the spring lacks depth and is too much fed by surface streams from without.

Through a poem should run a thread of emotional thought, strong enough to bind the parts together so vividly as to hold attention close to the substance. Many a so-called poem is but a string of elaborate stanzas, mostly of four lines each, too slightly connected to coöperate as members of an organic whole. There is not heat enough in the originating impulse to fuse the parts into unity. There is too much manufacture and not enough growth. Coleridge says, "The difference between manufactured poems and works of genius is not less than between an egg and an egg-shell; yet at a distance they both look alike."

Men without depth of sensibility or breadth of nature, but with enough sense of beauty to modulate their thoughts, using with skill the floating capital of sentiment and the current diction and molds of verse, for a generation are esteemed poets of more genius than they have, their pages being elaborate verse flavored with poetry, rather than poems. In much verse are found old thoughts re-dressed in the scoured garments of an ambitious fancy. The remark being made to Goethe in his latter days, that scarce one of the younger German poets had given an example of good prose, he rejoined, "That is very natural; he who would write prose must have something to say; but he who has nothing to say can make verses and rhymes; for one word gives the other, till at last you have before you what in fact is nothing, yet looks as though it were something." There is much good-looking verse which does not fulfill any one of Milton's primary conditions for poetry, being artificial instead of "simple," and having neither soul enough to be "passionate," nor body enough to be "sensuous." By passionate Milton means imbued with feeling.

The poetical mood is always a visionary mood; so much so, that even when the poet is depicting an actual person or scene, he must see it with the imaginative eye, the inward eye, as well as with the outward. Unless he does, there is no poetry in the result. A poem is twofold, presenting an actuality, and at the same time a tender lucent image thereof, like the reflection of a castle, standing on the edge of a lake, in the calm deep mirror before it: at one view we see the castle and its glistening counterpart. In the best poetry there is vivid picture-making: reality is made more visible by being presented as a beautiful show. It is the power to present the beautiful show which constitutes the poet. To conceive a scene or person with such liveliness and compactness as to be able to transfer the conception to paper with a distinctness and palpitation that shall make the reader behold in it a fresh and buoyant type of the actual — this implies a subtle, creative life in the mind, this is the test of poetic faculty. To stand this test there must be an inward sea of thought and sensibility, dipping into which the poet is enabled to hold up his conception or invention all adrip with sparkling freshness. The poetic mind, with a firm, and at the same time free, easy hold, holds a subject at arm's length, where it can be turned round in the light; the prosaic mind grasps and hugs what it handles so close that there is no room for play of light or motion.

Contemplating synthetically the highest and choicest and purest, and at the same time actively endeavoring to embody it, the genuine poet has in his best work joy as exalted as the mind can here attain to; and in the reader who can attune himself to the high pitch, he enkindles the same kind of joyful exaltation. There is current a detestable phrase or definition, which even Coleridge allows himself to countenance, namely, that poetry is something which gives pleasure. Pleasure! Do we speak of the pleasure of beholding the sun rise out of the Atlantic or from the top of Mount Washington, or the pleasure of standing beside Niagara, or of reading about the self-sacrifice of Regulus or Winkelried? Pleasure is a word limited to the animal or to the lighter feelings.

"Let me have the pleasure of taking wine with you." A good dinner gives great pleasure to a circle of gourmets. Even enjoyment, a higher word than pleasure, should, when applied to poetry, be conjoined with some elevating qualification; for all the feelings impart enjoyment through their simple healthy function, and there are people who enjoy a cock-pit, or a bull-fight, or an execution. But poetry causes that refined, super-sensuous delight which follows the apprehension of any thought, sentiment, act, or scene, which rises towards the best and purest possible in the range of that thought, sentiment, act, or scene. In the poetical there always is exaltation, a reaching towards perfection, a subtle, blooming spirituality. The end of poetry is not pleasure, — this were to speak too grossly, — but refined enjoyment through emotion.

To him who has the finer sensibility to become aware of its presence, the poetical is everywhere. The beautiful is a kiss which man gives to Nature, who returns it; to get the kiss from her he must first give it. Wordsworth says, "Poetry is the breath and fine spirit of all knowledge; it is the impassioned expression which is in the countenance of all science."

It might be called the aromatic essence of all life.

A poem is the incarnation of this aroma, the condensation of it into form. A drop of dew symbolizes a poem ; for a true poem should be oval, without angles, transparent, compact, complete in itself, graceful from inward quality and fullness. It may be of a few lines, or of hundreds or thousands ; but there must be no superfluous line or word. A poem drops out of the brain a fragrant distillation. A poem must be a spiritual whole ; that is, not only with the parts organized into proportioned unity, but with the whole and the parts springing out of the idea, the sentiment, form obedient to substance, body to soul, the sensuous life to the inward. For enduring, ruddy incarnation, the subject, whether it be incident, scene, sentiment, or action, must have within its core this essential aroma. The poet (and the test of his poetic capacity is his gift to draw the fragrance out of such a core) keeps his conception distinctly and vividly before him. The conception or ideal prefigurement of his theme precedes him, like the pillar of fire in the night, drawing him onward surely and rapidly. Otherwise he lags and flags and stumbles. The spring into poetry is on a flash, which not only lights up the thought on which it springs, but renews, re-creates it.

A man's chief aim in life should be to better himself, to keep bettering himself ; and in this high duty the poet helps him. Poetry is the great educator of the feelings. By seizing and holding up to view the noblest and cleanest and best there is in human life, poetry elevates and refines the feelings. It reveals and strengthens the spirituality of our nature. Poetry tunes the mind. Faculty of admiration is one of our super-animal privileges. Poetry purges and guides admiration ; and the sounder and higher our admirations, the more admirable ourselves become.

The best poetry turns the mind inward upon itself, and sweetens its imaginations. Our imaginations, that is, our inward thoughts, plans, shaping our silent, interior doings, these are the chief part of us ; for out of these come most of our outward acts, and all of their color. As is the preponderance of the man, will be this inward brood. The timid man will imagine dangers, the anxious man troubles, the hopeful man successes, the avaricious man accumulations, the ambitious possession of power ; and the poetic man will imagine all sorts of perfections, be ever yearning for a better and higher, be ever building beautiful air-castles, earthy or moral, material or ethereal, according as the sensuous or the spiritual predominates in his nature. Beckford, of a sensuously poetic nature, having command of vast wealth, brought his castle in the air down to the ground, and dazzled his contemporaries with Fonthill Abbey. Not only are Fonthill Abbeys and all beautiful buildings achieved through the warm action of the poetic faculty, but all improvements are brought about by its virtue. Out of this deep, inward, creative power issue all theories and practice for the bettering of human conditions. All original founders and discoverers are poets: the most poetic French mind I know is that of Fourier.

When a mind, having the texture and expansibility to become surcharged with magnetic effluence, has moreover that æsthetic gift of rhythmic expression which involves a sense of the beautiful, that is, of the high and exquisite possibilities of created things, — when such a mind, under the pressure of inward needs, betakes it to embodying in verse its imaginations and conceptions, the result is poetry. *Poetry is thought so inly warmed by creative sensibility as to overflow in musical cadence.* And when we consider that thought is the gathering of loose intellectual activity into a fast focus ; that creative sensibility is human feeling refined of its dross, stilled of its tumultuousness in the glow of the beautiful ; that musical cadence is heard by him who can hearken with such rapt reverence as to catch some sound of the tread in divine movement, we may apprehend that a genuine poem implies, for its conception, an illuminated plenitude of mind, and involves in its production a beatific visionariness.

III.

STYLE.

THOUGHT, act, and speech are of one substance. Where the best things have been done, the best things have been said. The history of Attica is richer and more significant than that of her sister-states of old Greece, and among them her literature is supreme. So of England in modern Europe. And where good thoughts have been uttered the form of those will be finest which carry the choicest life. The tree gets its texture from the quality of its sap. Were I asked what author is the most profitable to the student of English on account of style, I should answer, study Shakespeare.

Have something to say, and say it in the best and fewest words, were a good recipe for style. In this brief precept there are more ingredients than at first view appear. To have something to say implies that a man must write out of himself, and not chiefly out of his memory; and so to write involves much more than many people are aware of; in order that his style have freshness, which is a primary need of a good style, the writer's thought must be fresh. Then, to say his thought in the best and fewest words implies faculty of choice in words, and faculty of getting rid of all verbal superfluity; and these two faculties betoken proficiencies and some of the finer æsthetic forces.

Style itself is a gift (or more properly an issue of several gifts), not an acquisition; it cannot be taught. As to teaching style to one with inharmonious or defective natural powers, you might as well attempt to teach a thrush to sing the songs of the nightingale. To be sure, like the poetical, or the scientific, or any mental gift, it requires culture. But style is little helped from without. The most, as to the form of his utterance, that a writer can get from others — whether through study of the best masters or through direct rhetorical instruction — is in the mechanical portion of the art; that is, how to put sentences together according to relation of clauses, how by position of words and phrases to avoid obscurity and awkwardness, and thus make most presentable and accessible what he has to give out. Even in these superficial lessons success imports something more than a superficial capacity. These lessons learnt, and you have still to go behind them for style, whose cradle is within you. *Le stylê c'est l'homme même* (a man's style is his very self), is the oft-quoted profound sentence of Buffon. Style comes out of the interior: beneath a genuinely good style are secret springs which give to the surface its movement and sparkle. Mostly when people talk of style 't is of the surface; they think not of the depths beneath. In popularly good styles there are indeed no deep or fine springs beneath; in Tom Moore's, for example, or Southey's.

Nevertheless there are writers who have more skill and art than others in presenting agreeably what they have to say, in gracefully shaping their utterances; they are better endowed with some of the plastic faculties; they have what Sainte-Beuve calls the genius of style. Tact and craft enable them to make themselves more readable than some other writers of more substance; still, they are only capable of so doing by means of qualities which, however secondary, are interior and fervent, and the skill imparted by which cannot be acquired except through the presence of these qualities. This superiority of skill in form is illustrated by the literature of France in comparison with the literature of Germany, and even with that of England. The French follow a precept thus embodied by Béranger: "Perfection of style should be sought by all those who believe themselves called to diffuse useful thoughts. Style, which is only the form appropriated to a subject by art and reflection, is the passport of which every thought has need in order to circulate, expand, and lodge itself in people's brains. To neglect style is not to show sufficient love for the ideas one wishes to make others adopt." And so effective is the following of such a precept that, through careful devices and manipulating cleverness, a brilliant success, though transitory, is achieved by some writers who range lightly over surfaces, their thoughts dipping no deeper than a flat stone thrown to skim along the water, which it keeps ruffling, making a momentary sprightly splash at each contact, until, its force being soon spent, it disappears and is seen no more.

The possession of certain mental gifts constitutes a talent for writing, gifts which, with reference to the great primary powers of the mind, are secondary. Sainte-Beuve says of the Abbé Gerbet that he "had naturally the flowers of speech, movement and rhythm of phrase, measure and choice of expression, even figurative language, what, in short, makes a talent for writing." The possessor of these qualifications may, nevertheless, rise only a little above mediocrity. Of the styles of many, even clever, accomplished writers, one gets a clear notion from the remark made of a certain polished actress, that she always played well, never better.

When Sainte-Beuve says, *Rien ne vit que par le style,* he asserts in fact the exclusive privilege of original thought to give permanence to literary work; for nothing but an interior source can give life to expression. The inward flow will shape itself adequately and harmoniously in proportion as it has at full command the auxiliary, what I have called the plastic literary qualities; but shape itself it will, effectively and with living force, without the fullest command, while the readiest mastery over these qualities can never give vitality to style when are wanting primary resources. Literary substance which does not shape itself successfully (it may not be with the fullest success) is internally defective, is insufficient; for if it throb with life, it will mold a form for its embodiment, albeit that form, from lack of complete command of the secondary agents, will not be so graceful or rich as with such command it would have been. Wordsworth has made to English literature a permanent addition which is of the highest worth, in spite of notable plastic deficiencies. A conception that has a soul in it will find itself a body, and if not a literary body, one furnished by some other of the fine arts; or, wanting that, in practical enterprise or invention. And the body or form will be stamped with the inward lineaments of the man. Style issues from within, and if it does not, it is not style, but manner. Words get all their force from the thoughts and feelings behind them. They are necessary media, created, molded, and combined by mental wants. Picking and polishing words and phrases is ineffectual without the picking and polishing of the thoughts: below the surface of words lies that which controls and vivifies style. And then between the substance, the mental material, and the executive faculties there must be lively harmony. The executive power is a purely intellectual composite instrument; the force that wields it is feeling. For the best style the wielding force must be fine as well as rich and strong, and the shaping, harmonizing instrument of superfine temper and smiling willingness.

Style, in writing, is the art of putting into words what you think or feel, in such a way as to make the best of it — presupposed, that what you think or feel is worth putting into printed words. There are men who, without being original or inventive, have still, through strong understanding and culture, much to say that will profit their contemporaries ; men of a certain mental calibre, of talent, activity, will, cleverness, of verbal facility and of prominent ambition and in most cases of audacity, and who by discipline and labor attain to a style which for their purposes is effective. Of this class Jeffrey, Brougham, Macaulay are conspicuous examples. Theirs are not winged minds. They keep to the plane of commonplace ; they are never rapt into an upper sphere of thought, where sentences grow transparent, illuminated by soulful revelations. All three lack subtlety, the finer insight, a penetrating perception. The style of such men, even when most vivacious, is never marked by geniality, by newness of turns, by imaginative combinations, by rhythmical sweeps, and especially not by freshness, of all which the fountain is originality, genius, creativeness. It is related that after several of Carlyle's papers had appeared in the "Edinburgh Review," Brougham, one of its founders and controllers, protested that if that man were permitted to write any more he should cease to be a contributor. And so the pages of the Review were closed against the best writer it ever had. This arbitrary proceeding of Brougham is to be mainly accounted for as betraying the instinct of creeping talent in the presence of soaring genius.

Not less than men of talent men of genius need to cultivate style; nay, from the copiousness and variousness of their material, and from its very inwardness, the molds into which it is to be thrown need the finest care. Coleridge, rich and incomparable as he is, would have made many of his prose pages still more effective by a studious supervision; and De Quincey tells us what labor his periods sometimes cost him. The following advice, given in a letter from Maurice de Guérin to his sister, may be addressed to all literary aspirants: "Form for yourself a style which shall be the expression of yourself. Study our French language by attentive reading, making it your care to mark constructions, turns of expression, delicacies of style, but without ever adopting the manner of any master. In the works of these masters we must learn our language, but we must use it each in our own fashion."

One of the first constituents of a good style is what Coleridge calls "progressive transition," which implies a dynamic force, a propulsive movement, behind the pen. Hazlitt, for example, somewhat lacked this force, and hence De Quincey is justified to speak of his solitary flashes of thought, his "brilliancy, seen chiefly in separate splinterings of phrase or image, which throw upon the eye a vitreous scintillation for a moment." One of the charms, in a high sense, of Coleridge's page is that in him this dynamic force was present in liveliest action. His intellect, ever enkindled by his emotions, exacted logical sequence, and thus a rapid forward movement is overspread by a glow of generous feeling, which, being refined by his poetic sensibility made his style luminous and flowing.

De Quincey, treating of aphoristic writing, says, "Any man [he of course means any man with good things in him] as he walks through the streets may contrive to jot down an independent thought, a short-hand memorandum of a great truth; but the labor of composition begins when you have to put your separate threads of thought into a loom; to weave them into a continuous whole; to connect, to introduce them; to blow them out or expand them; to carry them to a close." Buffon attached the greatest importance to sequence, to close dependence, to continuous enchainment. He detested a chopped, jerky style, that into which the French are prone to fall. Certain it is, and from obvious causes, that much of the secret of style lies in aptness of sequence, thought and word, through an irresistible impulsion and pertinence, leaping forth nimbly, each taking its place promptly, because naturally and necessarily. Through fusion and close coherency and dependence, the flow is at once smooth and lively. The grace as well as the strength of the living physical body depends much, nay primarily, on the joints. So with the body of a good writer's thoughts, that is, his mode of utterance. To the linking of sentences and paragraphs (the links being self-wrought out of inward sap) is due much of the buoyancy and force of style. The springiness of the joints depends, in the body, on the quality of its nervous life; in style, much on the marrow and validity of the thoughts. By a sprightly stream of thought, fed from a full spring of feeling, the current of words is kept lively and graceful. Words, sentences, paragraphs, cannot be held closely, symmetrically, attractively together, without the unction invisibly distilled from brisk mental movement, movement starting from sentiment fresh and true. Soul is the source of style. Not sensibility alone is a prerequisite for style: the sensibility must be *active*, made active by the fine aspiring urgency which ever demands the best. A good style will have the sheen communicated by lubrication from within, not the gloss of outward rubbing.

That style varies in pitch and tone according to the subject treated ought to be self-evident. In every page of "The Merry Wives of Windsor" we recognize Shakespeare not less palpably than in "King Lear." In his "Recollections of Charles Lamb" De Quincey writes, "Far be it from me to say one word in praise of those — people of how narrow a sensibility — who imagine that a simple (that is, according to many tastes, an unelevated and *unrhythmical*) style — take, for instance, an Addisonian or a Swiftian style — is *unconditionally* good. Not so : all depends upon the subject ; and there is a style, transcending these and all other modes of simplicity, by infinite degrees, and, in the same proportion, impossible to most men, the rhythmical, the continuous — what in French is called the *soutenu* — which, to humbler styles stands in the relation of an organ to a shepherd's pipe. This also finds its justification in its subject ; and the subject which *can* justify it must be of a corresponding quality — loftier — and therefore, rare."

I quote De Quincey because he has written more, and more profoundly as well as more copiously, on style than any writer I know. To this point, — the adaption of style to subject, — he returns, laying down with clearness and truth the law which should here govern. In a paper on Schlosser's " Literary History of the Eighteenth Century " he reaffirms — what cannot be too strongly insisted on — the falsity of the common opinion that Swift's style is, for all writers, a model of excellence, showing how it is only fitted to the kind of subjects on which Swift wrote, and concluding with this characteristic passage: "That nearly all the blockheads with whom I have at any time had the pleasure of conversing upon the subject of style (and pardon me for saying that men of the most sense are apt, upon two subjects, viz., poetry and style, to talk *most* like blockheads) have invariably regarded Swift's style not as if *relatively*, (i. e., *given* a proper subject), but as if *absolutely* good —good unconditionally, no matter what the subject. Now, my friend, suppose the case, that the dean had been required to write a pendant for Sir Walter Raleigh's immortal apostrophe to Death, or to many passages in Sir Thomas Brown's 'Religio Medici' and his 'Urn-Burial,' or to Jeremy Taylor's inaugural sections of his 'Holy Living and Dying,' do you know what would have happened? Are you aware what sort of a ridiculous figure your poor bald Jonathan would have cut? About the same that would be cut by a forlorn scullion or waiter from a greasy eating-house at Rotterdam, if suddenly called away in vision to act as seneschal to the festival of Belshazzar the king, before a thousand of his lords."

That no writer of limited faculties can have a style of high excellence ought to be a truism. Through a certain equilibrium among his faculties, and assiduous literary culture, such a one may excel colleagues who move on the same bounded plane; but that is all. From the shallowest utterance, where, thoughts and feelings lying just below the surface, there can be no strong lights and shadows, no splendid play in the exposition, styles range, with the men who make them, through all degrees of liveliness and significance and power, up to that simple grandeur which conceals a vast volume of thought, and implies a divine ruling of multiplicity.

In a good style, on whatever degree it stands, there must be a full marriage between word and thought, so clean an adjustment of expression to material as to leave no rough edges or nodes. The words must not be too big or too shiny for the thought; they must not stand out from the texture, embossing, as it were, the matter. A style can hardly be too nervous; it can be too muscular, as, for example, was sometimes that of Michael Angelo in sculpture and painting.

A primary requisite for a good style is that the man and the writer be one; that is, that the man have a personal feeling for, a free sympathy with, the theme the writer has taken in hand;

his subject must be fitted to him, and he to his subject. That he be sincere is not enough; he must be cordial; then he will be magnetic, attractive. You must love your work to do it well.

A good style is a stream, and a lively stream: it flows ever onward actively. The worst vice a style can have is languor. With some writers a full stop is a double full stop: the reader does not get forward. Much writing consists of little more than sluggish eddies. In many minds there is not leap enough for a style. Excellence in style demands three vivacities, and rather exacting ones, for they involve a somewhat rare mental apportionment; the vivacities of healthy and poetic feeling, of intellectual nimbleness, and of inviolable sequence.

Writers there are who get to be partially self-enslaved by a routine of phrases and words under the repetition of which thought is hardened by its molds. Thence mechanical turns and forms, which cause numbness, even when there is a current of intellectual activity. Writers most liable to this subjection are they who have surrendered themselves to set opinions and systems, who therefore cease to grow, — a sad condition for man or writer.

Hypocrites in writing, as in talking and doing, end badly. A writer who through his style aims to seem better or other than himself is soon found out. The desire so to seem argues a literary incapacity ; it looks as though the very self — which will shine through the style — lacked confidence in its own substance. And after all, in writing as in doing and talking, a man must be himself, will be himself in spite of himself. One cannot put on his neighbor's style any more than he can put on his neighbor's limbs.

Not only has prose its melody as well as verse, but there is no *style* unless sentences are pervaded, I might say animated, by rhythm ; lacking appropriate movement, they are inelastic, inert, drowsy. Rhythm implies a soul behind it and in it. The best style will have a certain rotundity imparted by the ceaseless rocking of thought in the deep ocean of sentiment. Without some music in them sentences were torpid, impracticable. To put thoughts and words so together that there shall be a charm in the presentation of them, there needs a lively harmony among certain faculties, a rhythm in the mind. Hence Cicero said that to write prose well, one must be able to write verse. The utterance of music in song or tune, in artful melody or choral harmony, is but the consummation of a power which is ever a sweetener in life's healthily active exhibitions, the power of sound. Nature is alive with music. In the fields, in the air, sound is a token of life. On high, bare, or snow-covered mountains the sense of oppression comes in great part from the absence of sound. But stand in spring under a broad, sapful Norway maple, leafless as yet, its every twig and spray clad in tender green flowerets, and listen to the musical murmur of bees above you, full of life and promise, a heavenly harmony from unseen choristers. Here is a symbol of the creative energy, unceasing, unseen, and ever rhythmical.

The heartier and deeper the thought, the more melody will there be in its fit expression, and thence the higher range of style is only reached by poets, or by men who, though poetically minded, yet lack "the accomplishment of verse." The sudden electric injection of light into a thought or object or sentiment — in this consists the gift poetical, a gift which implies a sensibility so keen and select as to kindle the light, and an intellect fine and firm enough to hold and transmit it. A writer in whom there is no poetic feeling can hardly rise to a style. Whoever has tried to read a play of Scribe will understand from this why Sainte-Beuve affirms of him that he is utterly devoid of the faculty of style (*dénué de la faculté du style*). Contrast with Scribe his fellow-countryman, the great Molière. Thence, Joubert says, "Many of our poets having written in prose, ordinary style has received from them a brilliancy and audacities which it would not have had without them. Perhaps, too, some prose writers, who were born poets without being born versifiers, have contributed to adorn our language, even in its familiarities, with those riches and that pomp which until then had been the exclusive property of the poetic idiom."

A man of poetic sensibility is one born with a sleepless eye to the better, an ear that craves the musical, a soul that is uneasy in presence of the defective or the incomplete. This endowment implies a mind not only susceptible of the higher and finer movements of thought, but which eagerly demands them, and which thus makes the writer exacting towards himself. Hence only he attains to a genuine correctness; he was correct by instinct before he was so by discipline. In the whole as well as the parts he requires finish and proportion. Within him there is a momentum which fills out his thought and its worded envelope to warm convexity. Only he has the fine tact and discernment to know the full meaning of each word he uses. The best style is organic in its details as well as its structure; it shows modeling, a handling of words and phrases with the pliancy and plastic effects of clay in the hands of the sculptor. Goethe says that only poets and artists have method, because they require to see a thing before them in a completed, rounded form. Writing is a fine art, and one of the finest; and he who would be a master in this art must unite genial gifts with conscientious culture.

Of style the highest examples, therefore, are to be found in the verse of the great poets, of the deep rhythmic souls who make a sure, agile intellect their willing Ariel; and no prose writer gets to be a master in style but through kindred endowment. The compact, symmetrical combination of gifts and acquirements, of genius with talent, demanded for the putting forth of a fresh, priceless poem, this he need not have; but his perceptions must be brightened by the light whose fountain is the inward enjoyment of the more perfect in form, deed, and sentiment, and his best thoughts suffused with that fragrance whose only source is the ravishment of the beautiful.

IV.

DANTE AND HIS LATEST TRANSLATORS.[1]

"GHOSTS and witches are the best machinery for a modern epic." So said Charles Fox, who fed his imagination on verse of this aspiring class. Fox was no literary oracle, and his opinion is here cited only as evidence that the superearthly is an acknowledged element in the epopee. The term "machinery" implies ignorance of the import of the super-earthly in epic poetry, an ignorance attendant on materialism and a virtual unbelief. No poet who should accept the term could write an epic, with or without the "machinery." Such acceptance would betoken that weakness of the poetic pinion which surely follows a want of faith in the invisible supervisive energies.

A genuine epic, of the first class, is a world-poem, a poem of depth and height and breadth, narrating long-prepared ruin or foundation of a

[1] Putnam's Magazine, 1868.

race; and poetry, soaring beyond history, is bold to lay bare the method of the divine intervention in the momentous work. The epic poet, worthy of the lofty task, has such large sympathies, together with such consciousness of power, that he takes on him to interpret and incarnate the celestial coöperation. There are people, and some of them even poets, whose consciousness is so smothered behind the senses, that they come short of belief in spiritual potency. They are what, with felicity of phrase, Mr. Matthew Arnold calls —

> "Light half-believers in our casual creeds."

Homer and Milton were believers: they believed in the visible, active presence on the earth of the god Mars, and the archangel Raphael. Had they not, there would have been no "Iliad," no "Paradise Lost."

Dante, too, was a believer; and such warm, wide sympathies had he, and an imagination so daring, that he undertook to unfold the divine judgment on the multitudinous dead, ranging with inspired vision through hell, and purgatory, and heaven. In his large, hot heart, he lodged the racy, crude beliefs of his age, and with poetic pen wrought them into immortal shapes. The then religious imaginations of Christendom, positive, and gross, and very vivid; the politics of Italy, then tumultuous and embittered; the theology and philosophy of his time, fantastic, unfashioned — all this was his material. But all this, and were it ten times as much, is but the skeleton, the frame. The true material of a poem is the poet's own nature and thoughts, his sentiment and his judgment, his opinions, aspirations, imaginations, his veriest self, the whole of him, especially the best of him.

Than imaginary journeys through the realms beyond the grave, which were so much the vogue with the religious writers of the day, — and literature then was chiefly, almost exclusively, religious, — no more broad or tempting canvas could be offered to a poet, beset, as all poets are apt to be, with the need of utterance, and possessed, moreover, of a graphic genius that craved strong, glowing themes for its play. The present teeming world to be transfigured into the world to come, and the solicitation and temptation to do this brought to a manly, powerful nature, passionate, creative, descriptive, to a stirring realist, into whose breast, as a chief actor on the Italian scene, ran, all warm from the wheels of their spinning, the threads of Italian politics at the culmination of the papal imperial conflict; and that breast throbbing with the fiery passions of republican Italy, while behind the throb beat the measure of a poetic soul impelled to tune the wide, variegated cacophony. Proud, passionate, and baffled, the man Dante deeply swayed the poet. Much of his verse is directly woven out of his indignations and burning personal griefs. At times, contemporaneous history tyrannized over him.

Dante's high and various gifts, his supreme poetic gift, the noble character and warm individuality of the man, with the pathos of his personal story, the full, lively transcript he hands down of the theology and philosophy of his age, his native literary force as molder of the Italian language, his being the bold, adventurous initiator, the august father of modern poetry — all this has combined to keep him and his verse fresh in the minds of men through six centuries. But even all this would not have made him one of the three or four world-poets, would not have won for him the wreath of universal European translation. What gave his rare qualities their most advantageous field, not merely for the display of their peculiar superiorities, but for keeping their fruit sound and sweet, was that he is the historian of hell, purgatory, and heaven — of the world to come such as it was pictured in his day, and as it has been pictured more or less ever since — the word-painter of that visionary, awful hereafter, the thought of which has ever been a spell.

Those imaginations as to future being — to the Middle Ages so vivid as to become soul-realities — Dante, with his transcendent pictorial mastership, clothed in words fresh and weighty from the mine of popular speech, stamping them with his glittering imperial superscription. Imaginations! there are imaginations of the future, the reverse of poetical. Hunger will give you tormenting imaginations of breakfasts and dinners; avarice enlivens some minds with pictures of gains that are to be. But imaginations of the life beyond the grave, these we cannot entertain without spirituality. The having them with any urgency and persistence implies strong spiritual prepossessions: men must be self-possessed with their higher self, with their spirit. The very attempt to figure your disembodied state is an attempt poetical. To succeed with any distinctness denotes some power of creative projection: without wings, this domain cannot be entered. In Dante's time these attempts were common. Through his preëminent qualifications, crowned with the poetic faculty, the faculty of sympathy with ideal excellence, his attempt was a great, a unique success.

To accompany Dante through his vast triple trans-terrestrial world, would seem to demand in the reader a sustained effort of imagination. But Dante is so graphic, and, we might add, corporeal in his pictures, puts such a pulse into his figures, that the artistic illusion wherewith we set out is exchanged for, or rather overborne by, an illusion of the reality of what is represented. Yet from the opening of the first canto he is ever in the super-earthly world, and every line of the fourteen thousand has the benefit of a super-earthly, that is, a poetic atmosphere, which lightens it, transfigures it, floats it. One reads with the poetic prestige of the knowledge that every scene is trans-terrestrial; and, at the same time, every scene is presented with a physical realism, a visual and audible vividness, which captivates and holds the perceptive faculty; so that the reader finds himself grasped, as it were, in a vice, whose double handle is mortised on one side in the senses, and on the other in the spiritual imagination.

Dante had it in him, — this hell, purgatory, and heaven — so full and warm and large was his nature. Within his own breast he had felt, with the keen intensity of the poetic temperament, the loves and hates, the griefs and delights of life. Through his wealth of heart he had a fellow-feeling for all the joys and sorrows of his brother-men, and, added to this, an artist's will and want to reproduce them, and *to* reproduce them a clear, outwelling, intellectual vivacity. He need scarcely have told us that his poem, though treating of spirits, relates to the passions and doings of men in the flesh. He chose a theme that at once seized the attention of his readers, and gave to himself a boundless scope. His field was all past history, around the altitudes of which are clustered biographical traits and sketches of famous sinners and famous saints, of heroes and lofty criminals; and, along with this, contemporaneous Florentine and Italian history, with its tumults and vicissitudes, its biographies and personalities, its wraths and triumphs.

Dante exhibits great fertility in situations

and conjunctions; but, besides that many of them were ready to his hand, this kind of inventiveness denotes of itself no fine creative faculty. It is the necessary equipment of the voluminous novelist. In this facility and abundance Goldsmith could not have coped with James and Bulwer; and yet the "Vicar of Wakefield" (not to go so high as "Tristram Shandy" and "Don Quixote") is worth all their hundred volumes of tales put together. What insight, what weight, and faithfulness, and refinement, and breadth, and truth, and elevation of character and conception, does the framework of incident support and display? That is the æsthetic question. The novels of every day bristle with this material inventiveness, this small, abounding, tangled underwood of event and sensation, which yields no timber and wherein birds will not build. The invention exhibited in the punishments and tortures and conditions of the "Inferno" and "Purgatorio" and "Paradiso," is not admirable for their mere exuberance and diversity, — for that might have come from a comparatively prosaic mind, especially when fed, as all minds then were, with the passionate mediæval beliefs, — but for the heart there is in them, throbbing deeply in some, and for the human sympathy, and thence, in part, the photographic fidelity, and for the paramount gift poetically to portray.

A consequence of the choice of subject, and, as regards the epic quality of Dante's poem, an important consequence, is that there is in it no unity of interest. The sympathies of the reader are not engrossed by one great group of characters, acting and reacting on one another through the whole sweep of the invention. Instead of this, we have a long series of unconnected pictures, each one awakening a new interest. Hereby the mind is distracted, the attention being transferred at every hundred lines to a fresh figure or group. We pass through a gallery of pictures and portraits, classed, to be sure, by subjects, but distinct one from the other, and separated by the projection of as many different frames. We are on a weird, adventurous journey, and make but brief stops, however attractive the strangers or acquaintance we meet. We go from person to person, from scene to scene; so that at the end of the journey, although the perception has been richly crowded, one impression has effaced the other. Not carrying the weight, not pulsating in its every limb with the power of a broad, deep, involved story, architecturally reared on one foundation, whose parts are all subordinated to a great unity, the "Divina Commedia," as an organic, artistic whole, is inferior to the "Iliad" and "Paradise Lost," and to the Grecian and Shakespearean tragedies.

The exclusive super-earthliness of his scenes and personages, and, with this, his delight in picture-drawing, keep Dante close to his page — fastened to it, we might say, by a twofold fascination. Among the many faculties that equip him for his extraordinary task, most active is that of form. Goethe says of him, "The great intellectual and moral qualities of Dante being universally acknowledged, we shall be furthered in a right estimate of his works, if we keep in view that just in his life-time — Giotto being his contemporary — was the re-birth of plastic art in all its natural strength. By this sensuous, form-loving spirit of the age, working so widely and deeply, Dante, too, was largely swayed. With the eye of his imagination he seized objects so distinctly that he could reproduce them in sharp outline. Thence we see before us the most abstruse and unusual, drawn, as it were, after nature." In recognition of the same characteristic, Coleridge says, "In picturesqueness Dante is beyond all other poets, ancient or modern, and more in the stern style of Pindar than of any other. Michael Angelo is said to have made a design for every page of the 'Divina Commedia.'"

Dante, eminent in poetic gifts, has many sides, but this is his strongest side: he is preëminently a poet of form. In his mind and in his work there is a southern, an Italian, sensuousness. He is a poet of thought, but more a poet of molds; he is a poet of sentiment, but more a poet of pictures. Rising readily to generalization, still his intellect is more specific than generic. His subject — chosen by the concurrence of his æsthetic, moral, and intellectual needs — admits of, nay, demands portraits, isolated sketches, unconnected delineations. The personages of his poem are independent one of the other, and are thence the more easily drawn. Nor does Dante abound in transferable passages, sentences of universal application, from being saturated with the perfumed essence of humanity. We say it with diffidence, but to us it seems that there is a further poetic glance, more idealized fidelity, in Milton; more significance and wisdom and profound hint in Goethe. In Milton the mental reverberation is wider: he rivets us through distant grand association, by great suggestion. Thus, describing the darkened head of Satan, Milton says, —

> "As when the sun new risen
> Looks through the horizontal misty air,
> Shorn of his beams, or from behind the moon,
> In dim eclipse, disastrous twilight sheds
> On half the nations,"

Setting aside the epithets "horizontal" and "disastrous," which are poetically imaginative, the likening of Satan to the sun seen through a mist, or in eclipse, is a direct, parallel comparison that aids us to see Satan; and it is in such, immediate, not mediate, — not involving likeness between physical and mental qualities, but merely between physical, not between subtle, relations, — that Dante chiefly deals, showing imaginative fertility, helpful, needful to the poet, but different from, and altogether inferior to, poetic imagination. The mind attains to the height of poetic imagination when the intellect, urged by the purer sensibilities in alliance with aspiration for the perfect, exerts its imaginative power to the utmost, and, as the result of this exertion, discovers a thought or image which, from its originality, fitness, and beauty, gives to the reader a new delight. Of this, the lordliest mental exhibition, there is a sovereign example in the words wherewith Milton concludes the passage —

> "and with fear of change
> Perplexes monarchs."

This fills the mind with the terror he wishes his Satan to inspire; this gives its greatness to the passage.

Dante, by the distinctness of his outline, addresses himself more to the reader's senses and perception; Milton rouses his higher imaginative capacity. In the whole "Inferno," is there a sentence so aglow as this line and a half of "Paradise Lost"?

> "And the torrid clime
> Smote on him sore besides, vaulted with fire."

Or is there in Dante any sound so loud and terrible as that shout of Milton's demon-host —

> "That tore Hell's concave, and beyond
> Frighted the reign of Chaos and old Night"?

Here the unity of his theme stands Milton in stead for grandeur and breadth.

Dante is copious in similes. Such copiousness by no means proves poetic genius; and a superior poet may have less command of similes than one inferior to him. Wordsworth has much less of this command than Moore. But when a poet does use similes, he will be likely often to put of his best into them, for they are captivating instruments and facilities for poetic expansion. When a poet is in warm sympathy with the divine doings, there will be at times a flashing fitness in his similitudes, which are then the sudden offspring of finest intuition. In citing some of the most prominent in the "Divina Commedia," we at once give brief samples of Dante and of the craft of his three latest translators, using the version of Dr. Parsons for extracts from the "Inferno," that of Mr. Dayman for those from the "Purgatorio," and that of Mr. Longfellow for those from the "Paradiso."

"As well-filled sails, which in the tempest swell,
Drop, with folds flapping, if the mast be rent;
So to the earth that cruel monster fell,
And straightway down to Hell's Fourth Pit he went."

Inferno: Canto VII.

"Swept now amain those turbid waters o'er
A tumult of a dread portentous kind,
Which rocked with sudden spasms each trembling shore,
Like the mad rushing of a rapid wind;
As when, made furious by opposing heats,
Wild through the wood the unbridled tempest scours,
Dusty and proud, the cringing forest beats,
And scatters far the broken limbs and flowers;
Then fly the herds, — the swains to shelter scud.
Freeing mine eyes, 'Thy sight,' he said, 'direct
O'er the long-standing scum of yonder flood,
Where, most condense, its acrid streams collect.'"

Inferno: Canto IX.

"When, lo! there met us, close beside our track,
  A troop of spirits. Each amid the band
Eyed us, as men at eve a passer-by
  'Neath a new moon; as closely us they scanned,
As an old tailor doth a needle's eye."

Inferno: Canto XV.

"And just as frogs that stand, with noses out
  On a pool's margin, but beneath it hide
Their feet and all their bodies but the snout,
  So stood the sinners there on every side."

Inferno: Canto XXII.

"A cooper's vessel, that by chance hath been
  Either of middle-piece or cant-piece reft,
Gapes not so wide as one that from his chin
  I noticed lengthwise through his carcass cleft."

Inferno: Canto XXVIII.

"We tarried yet the ocean's brink upon,
  Like unto people musing of their way,
Whose body lingers when the heart hath gone;
  And lo! as near the dawning of the day,
Down in the west, upon the watery floor,
  The vapor-fogs do Mars in red array,
Even such appeared to me a light that o'er
  The sea so quickly came, no wing could match
Its moving. Be that vision mine once more."

Purgatorio: Canto II.

"And thou, remembering well, with eye that sees
  The light, wilt know thee like the sickly one
That on her bed of down can find no ease,
  But turns and turns again her ache to shun."

Purgatorio: Canto VI.

"'T was now the hour the longing heart that bends
In voyagers, and meltingly doth sway,
Who bade farewell at morn to gentle friends ;
And wounds the pilgrim newly bound his way
With poignant love, to hear some distant bell
That seems to mourn the dying of the day ;
When I began to slight the sounds that fell
Upon my ear, one risen soul to view,
Whose beckoning hand our audience would compel."

Purgatorio: Canto VIII.

"There I the shades see hurrying up to kiss
Each with his mate from every part, nor stay,
Contenting them with momentary bliss.
So one with other, all their swart array
Along, do ants encounter snout with snout,
So haply probe their fortune and their way."

Purgatorio: Canto XXVI.

"Between two viands, equally removed
And tempting, a free man would die of hunger
Ere either he could bring unto his teeth.
So would a lamb between the ravenings
Of two fierce wolves stand fearing both alike ;
And so would stand a dog between two does.
Hence, if I held my peace, myself I blame not,
Impelled in equal measure by my doubts,
Since it must be so, nor do I commend."

Paradiso: Canto IV.

"And as a lute and harp, accordant strung
With many strings, a dulcet tinkling make
To him by whom the notes are not distinguished,
So from the lights that there to me appeared

Upgathered through the cross a melody,
  Which rapt me, not distinguishing the hymn."
Paradiso: Canto XIV.

" As through the pure and tranquil evening air
  There shoots from time to time a sudden fire,
Moving the eyes that steadfast were before,
  And seems to be a star that changeth place,
Except that in the part where it is kindled
  Nothing is missed, and this endureth little;
So from the horn that to the right extends
  Unto that cross's foot there ran a star
Out of the constellation shining there."
Paradiso: Canto XV.

'Even as remaineth splendid and serene
  The hemisphere of air, when Boreas
Is blowing from that cheek where he is mildest,
  Because is purified and resolved the rack
That erst disturbed it, till the welkin laughs
  With all the beauties of its pageantry;
Thus did I likewise, after that my lady
  Had me provided with a clear response,
And like a star in Heaven the truth was seen."
Paradiso: Canto XXVIII.

The first question to ask in regard to a simile found in verse is, Is it poetical? Is there, as effect of its introduction, any heightening of the reader's mood, any cleansing of his vision, any clarification of the medium through which he is looking? Is there a sudden play of light that warms, and, through this warmth, illuminates the object before him? Few of those just quoted, put to such test, could be called more than conventionally poetical — if this be not a solecism. To illustrate one sensuous object by another does not animate the mind enough to fulfill any one of the above conditions. Such similitudes issuing from intellectual liveliness, there is through them no steeping of intellectual perception in emotion. They may help to make the object ocularly more apparent, but they do not make the feeling a party to the movement. When this is done, — as in the examples from Canto XV. of the "Inferno," and Canto VIII. of the "Purgatorio," — what an instantaneous vivification of the picture!

But in the best of them the poetic gleam is not so unlooked-for bright as in the best of Shakespeare's. As one instance out of many: towards the end of the great soliloquy of Henry V., after enumerating the emblems and accompaniments of royalty, the king continues, —

> "No, not all these, thrice-gorgeous ceremony,
> Not all these, laid in bed majestical,
> Can sleep so soundly as the wretched slave;
> Who, with a body filled, and vacant mind,
> Gets him to rest, crammed with distressful bread;
> Never sees horrid night, the child of hell;
> But, like a lackey, from the rise to set,

> Sweats in the eye of Phœbus, and all night
> Sleeps in Elysium; next day, after dawn,
> Doth rise *and help Hyperion to his horse*."

What a sudden filling of the earth with light through that image, so fresh and unexpected, of the rising sun, with its suggestion of beauty and healthfulness! Then the far-reaching, transfiguring imagination, that, in a twinkle, transmutes into the squire of Hyperion a stolid rustic, making him suddenly radiant with the glory of morning. It is by this union of unexpectedness with fitness, of solidity with brilliancy, of remoteness with instantaneous presence, in his figures, denoting overflow of resources, a divine plenitude, so that we feel after Shakespeare has said his best things, that he could go on saying more and better, — it is especially by this lustrous, ever-teeming fullness of life, this creative readiness, that Shakespeare throws a farther and whiter and a broader light than Dante. Nor does Dante's page glisten, as Shakespeare's so often does, with metaphor, or compressed similes, that at times with a word open the spiritual sphere; not super-imposed as cold ornament, but inter-tissued with the web of thought, upflashings from a deep sea of mind, to quiver on the surface, as on the calm level of the Atlantic you may see a circuit of shining ripple, caused by schools of fish that have come up from the wealth in the depths below to help the sun to glisten, — a sign of life, power, and abundance.

Like his great compeer, Milton, Dante fails of universality from want of humor. Neither had any fun in him. This was the only fault (liberally to interpret Can's conduct) that Dante's host, Can Grande of Verona, had to find with him. The subjects of both poets (unconsciously chosen perhaps from this very defect of humor) were predominantly religious, and their theology, which was that of their times, was crude and cruel. The deep, sympathetic earnestness, which is the basis of the best humor, they had, but, to use an illustration of Richter, they could not turn sublimity upside down, — a great feat, only possible through sense of the comic, which, in its highest manifestation of humor, pillows pain in the lap of absurdity, throws such rays upon affliction as to make a grin to glimmer through gloom, and, with the fool in "Lear," forces you, like a child, to smile through warmest tears of sympathy. Humor imparts breadth and buoyancy to tolerance, enabling it to dandle lovingly the faults and follies of men; through humor the spiritual is calm and clear enough to sport with and toss the sensual; it is a compassionate, tearful delight; in its finest mood, an angelic laughter,

Of pathos Dante has given examples unsurpassed in literature. By the story of Ugolino the chords of the heart are so thrilled that pity and awe possess us wholly; and by that of Francesca they are touched to tenderest sympathy. But Ugolino is to Lear what a single fire-freighted cloud that discharges five or six terrific strokes is to a night-long tempest, wherein the thundering heavens gape with a hundred flashes.

All the personages of Dante's poem (unless we regard himself as one) are spirits. Shakespeare, throughout his many works, gives only a few glimpses into the world beyond the grave; but how grandly by these few is the imagination expanded. Clarence's dream, "lengthened after life," in which he passes "the melancholy flood," is almost super-Dantesque, concentrating in a few ejaculative lines a fearful foretaste of trans-earthly torment for a bad life on earth. And the great ghost in "Hamlet," when you read of him, how shadowy real! Dante's representation of disembodied humanity is too pagan, too palpable, not ghostly enough, not spiritualized with hope and awe.

Profound, awakening, far-stretching, much enfolding, thought-breeding thoughts, that can only grow in the soil of pure, large sensibilities, and by them are cast up in the heave and glow of inward motion, to be wrought by intellect and shaped in the light of the beautiful, — of these, which are the test of poetic greatness, Dante, if we may venture to say so, has not more or brighter examples than Milton, and not so many as Goethe; while of such passages, compactly embodying as they do the finer insights of a poetic mind, there are more in a single one of the greater tragedies of Shakespeare, than in all the three books of the "Divina Commedia."

Juxtaposition beside Shakespeare, even if it bring out the superiorities of the English bard, is the highest honor paid to any other great poet. Glory enough is it if admiration can lift Dante so high as to take him into the same look that beholds Shakespeare; what though the summit of the mighty Englishman shine alone in the sky, and the taller giant carry up towards heaven a larger bulk and more varied domains. The traveler, even if he come directly from wondering at Mont Blanc in its sublime presence, will yet stand with earnest delight before the majesty of the Yungfrau and the Eigher.

But it is time to speak of Dante in English.

"It were as wise to cast a violet into a crucible, that you might discover the formal principle of its color and odor, as to seek to transfuse from one language into another the creations of a poet." Thus writes a great poet, Shelley, in his beautiful "Defense of Poetry." But have we not in modern tongues the creations of Homer, and of Plato, who Shelley, on the same page, says is essentially a poet? And can we estimate the loss the modern mind would suffer by deprivation of them in translated form? Pope's Homer — still Homer though so Popish — has been a not insignificant chapter in the culture of thousands, who without it would have known no more of Hector and Achilles and the golden glowing cloud of passion and action through which they are seen superbly shining, than what a few of them would incidently have learnt from Lempriere. Lord Derby's Iliad has gone through many editions already. And Job and the Psalms: what should we have done without them in

English? Translations are the telegraphic conductors that bring us great messages from those in other lands and times, whose souls were so rich and deep that from their words their fellow-men, in all parts of the globe, draw truth and wisdom forever. The flash on which the message was first launched has lost some of its vividness by the way; but the purport of the message we have distinctly, and the joy or grief wherewith it is freighted, and even much of its beauty. Shall we not eat oranges, because on being translated from Cuba to our palates they have lost somewhat of their flavor?

In reading a translated poem we wish to have as much of the essence of the original, that is, as much of the poetry, as possible. A poem it is we sit down to read, not a relation of facts, or an historical or critical or philosophical or theological exposition, — a poem, only in another dress. Thence a work in verse, that has poetic quality enough to be worth translating, must be made to lose by the process as little as may be of its worth; and its worth every poem owes entirely to its poetic quality and the degree of that. A prose translation of a poem is an æsthetic impertinence. Shakespeare was at first opened to the people of the Continent in prose, because there was not then culture enough to reproduce him in verse. And in Shakespeare there is so much practical sense, so much telling comment on life, so much wit, such animal spirits, such touching stories so well told, that the great gain of having him even in prose concealed the loss sustained by the absence of rhythmic sound, and by the discoloration (impallidation, we should say, were the word already there) of hundreds of liveliest tinted flowers, the deflowering of many delicate stems. Forty years ago, Mr. Hayward translated the "Faust" of Goethe into prose; but let any one compare the Hymn of the Archangels and other of the more highly-wrought passages, as rendered by him, with any of the better translations in verse, — with that of Mr. Brooks for example, — to perceive at once the insufficiency, the flatness and meagreness of even so verbally faithful a prose version. The effect on "Faust," or on any high passionate poem, of attempting to put it into prose, is akin to what would be the effect on an exquisite *bas-relief* of reducing its projection one half by a persevering application of pumice. In all genuine verse (that is, in all poetic verse) the substance is so inwrought into the form and sound, that if in translating you entirely disregard these, rejecting both rhyme and measure, you subject the verse to a second depletion right upon that which it has to suffer by the transplanting of it into another soil.

The translator of a poem has a much higher and subtler duty than just to take the words and through them attempt passively to render the page into his own language. He must brace himself into an active state, a creative mood, the most creative he can command, then transport himself into the mind and mental attitude of the poet he would translate, feeling and seeing as the poet saw and felt. To get into the mood out of which the words sprang, he should go behind the words, embracing them from within, not merely seizing them from without. Having imbued himself with the thought and sentiment of the original, let him, if he can, utter them in a still higher key. Such surpassing excellence would be the truest fidelity to the original, and any cordial poet would especially rejoice in such elevation of his verse; for the aspiring writer will often fall short of his ideal, and to see it more nearly approached by a translator who has been kindled by himself, to find some delicate new flower revealed in a nook which he had opened, could not but give him a delight akin to that of his own first inspirations.

A poem, a genuine poem, assumes its form by an inward necessity. "Paradise Lost," conceived in Milton's brain, could not utter itself in any other mode than the unrhymed harmonies that have given to our language a new music. It could not have been written in the Spenserian stanza. What would the "Fairy Queen" be in blank verse? For his theme and mood Dante felt the need of the delicate bond of rhyme, which enlivens musical cadence with sweet reiteration. Rhyme was then a new element in verse, a modern æsthetic creation; and it is a help and an added beauty, if it be not obtrusive and too self-conscious, and if it be not a target at which the line aims; for then it becomes a clog to freedom of movement, and the pivot of factitious pauses, that are offensive both to sense and to ear. Like buds that lie half-hidden in leaves, rhymes should peep out, sparkling but modest, from the cover of words, falling on the ear as though they were the irrepressible strokes of a melodious pulse at the heart of the verse.

The *terza rima* — already in use — Dante adopted as suitable to continuous narrative,

With his feeling and æsthetic want rhymed verse harmonized, the triple repetition offering no obstacle, Italian being copious in endings of like sound. His measure is iambic, free iambic, and every line consists, not of ten syllables, but of eleven, his native tongue having none other than feminine rhymes. And this weakness is so inherent in Italian speech, that every line even of the blank verse in all the twenty-two tragedies of Alfieri ends femininely, that is, with an unaccented eleventh syllable. In all Italian rhyme there is thus always a double rhyme, the final syllable, moreover, invariably ending with a vowel. This, besides being too much rhyme and too much vowel, is, in iambic lines, metrically a defect, the eleventh syllable being a superfluous syllable.

In these two prominent features English verse is different from Italian: it has feminine rhymes, but the larger part of its rhymes are masculine; and it has fewer than Italian. This second characteristic, the comparative fewness of rhymes, is likewise one of its sources of strength: it denotes musical richness and not poverty, as at first aspect it seems to do, the paucity of like-sounding syllables implying variety in its sounds. It has all the vocalic syllables and endings it needs for softness, and incloses them mostly in consonants for condensation, vigor, and emphasis.

Primarily the translator has to consider the resources and individualities of his own tongue. In the case of Dante the rhythmical basis is the same in both languages; for the iambic measure is our chief poetic vehicle, wrought to perfection by Shakespeare and Milton. There only remains, then, rhyme and the division into stanzas. Can the *terza rima*, as used by Dante, be called a stanza? The lines are not separated into trios, but run into one another, clinging very properly to the rhymes, which, interlinking all the stanzas by carrying the echo still onward, bind each canto into one whole, just as our Spenserian form does each stanza into a whole of nine lines. Whether stanzas, strictly speaking, or not, shall we say our mind frankly about the *terza rima?* To us it seems not deserving of admiration *for its own sake;* and we surmise that had it not been consecrated by Dante, neither Byron nor Shelley would have used it for original poems. We are not aware that Dante's example has been followed by any poet of note in Italy. *Terza rima* keeps the attention suspended too long, keeps it ever on the stretch for something that is to come, and never does come, until at the end of the canto, namely, the last rhyme. The rhymes cannot be held down, but are ever escaping and running ahead. It looks somewhat like an artificial contrivance of the first rhymers of an uncultivated age. But Dante used it for his great song; and there it stands forever, holding in its folds the "Divina Commedia."

Now, in rendering into English the poem of Dante, is it essential, — in order to fulfill the conditions of successful poetic translation, — to preserve the triple rhyme? Not having in English a corresponding number of rhymes, will not the translator have to resort to transpositions, substitutions, forcings, indirections, in order to compass the meaning and the poetry? Place the passages already cited from Mr. Dayman beside the original, and the reader will be surprised to see how direct and literal, how faithful at once to the Italian thought and to English idiom in expressing it, Mr. Dayman is. His harness of triplets seems hardly to constrain his movement, so skillfully does he wear it. If we confront him with the spirited version in quatrains of Dr. Parsons, in the passages cited from the "Inferno," or with those from the "Paradiso," in Mr. Longfellow's less free unrhymed version, the resources and flexibility of Mr. Dayman in handling the difficult measure will be again manifest. To enable our readers to compare the translations with the original and with one another, we will give the Italian, and then the three versions, of the latter part of the Francesca story, from Canto V. of the "Inferno:" —

"Poi mi rivolsi a loro, e parlai io,
  E cominciai: Francesca, i tuoi martiri
A lagrimar mi fanno tristo, e pio.
  Ma dimmi: al tempo de' dolci sospiri,
A che, e come concedette Amore
  Che conosceste i dubbiosi desiri?
Ed ella a me: nessun maggior dolore,
  Che ricordarsi del tempo felice
Nella miseria, e ciò sa 'l tuo dottore.
  Ma se a conoscer la prima radice
Del nostro amor tu hai cotanto affetto,
  Farò come colui che piange, e dice.
Noi leggevamo un giorno per diletto
  Di Lancilotto, come Amor lo strinse.
Soli eravamo, e senza alcun sospetto.
  Per più fiate gli occhi ci sospinse
Quella lettura, e scolorocci 'l viso:
  Ma solo un punto fu quel, che ci vinse.
Qando leggemmo il disiato riso
  Esser baciato da cotanto amante,
Questi, che mai da me non sia diviso,
  La bocca mi baciò tutto tremante.
Galeotto fu il libro, e chi lo scrisse:
  Quel giorno più non vi leggemmo avante.

Mentre che l'uno spirito queste disse,
  L'altro piangeva si, che di pietade
Io venni meno come s'io morisse,
  E caddi, come corpo morto cade."

Mr. Dayman: —

" Then toward them turned again: 'Thy racking woe,'
  I said, 'Francesca, wrings from out mine eyes
The pious drops that sadden as they flow.
  But tell me, in your hour of honeyed sighs,
By whom and how love pitying broke the spell,
  And in your doubtful longings made too wise.'
And she to me: 'No keener pang hath hell,
  Than to recall, amid some deep distress,
Our happier time: thy teacher knows it well.
  Yet if desire so strong thy soul possess
To trace the root from whence our love was bred,
  His part be mine, who tells and weeps no less.
'T was on a day when we for pastime read
  Of Lancillot, how love snared him to ruin:
We were alone, nor knew suspicious dread.
  Oft on that reading paused our eyes, renewing
Their glance; and from our cheeks the color started;
  But one sole moment wrought for our undoing:
When that we read of lover so kind-hearted
  Kissing the smile so coveted before,
He that from me shall never more be parted
  Kissed me with lip to lip, trembling all o'er.
The broker of our vows, it was the lay,
  And he who wrote — that day we read no more.'
The other spirit, while the first did say
  These words, so moanèd, that with soft remorse
As death had stricken me, I swooned away,
  And down I fell, heavily as falls a corse."

Mr. Longfellow :—

"Then unto them I turned me, and I spake,
And I began : 'Thine agonies, Francesca,
Sad and compassionate to weeping make me.
But tell me, at the time of those sweet sighs,
By what and in what manner Love conceded
That you should know your dubious desires ?'
And she to me : 'There is no greater sorrow
Than to be mindful of the happy time
In misery, and that thy Teacher knows.
But if to recognize the earliest root
Of love in us thou hast so great desire,
I will do even as he who weeps and speaks.
One day we reading were for our delight
Of Launcelot, how Love did him enthrall.
Alone we were, and without any fear.
Full many a time our eyes together drew
That reading, and drove the color from our faces ;
But one point was it that o'ercame us.
Whenas we read of the much-longed-for smile
Being by such a noble lover kissed,
This one, who ne'er from me shall be divided,
Kissed me upon the mouth all palpitating.
Galeotto was the book and he who wrote it.
That day no farther did we read therein.'
And all the while one spirit uttered this,
The other one did weep so, that, for pity,
I swooned away as if I had been dying,
And fell even as a dead body falls."

Dr. Parsons :—

"Then, turning round to them, I thus began :
'Francesca ! tears must overflow mine eyes :
My pitying soul thy martyr-throes unman ;

But tell me, — in the time of happy sighs,
Your vague desires how gave Love utterance first?"
And she to me: "The mightiest of all woes
Is, in the midst of misery, to be cursed
With bliss remembered, — this thy teacher knows.
Yet, wouldst thou learn our passion's root and head,
As one may speak whose eyes with tears are dim,
So will I speak. Together once we read
The tale of Lancelot, — how Love bound him.
Alone we were without suspecting aught:
Oft in perusal paled our cheeks their hue,
And oft our eyes each other's glances caught;
But one sole passage 't was which both o'erthrew.
At reading of the longed-for smile, — to be
By such a lover's kissing so much blest,
This dearest — never shalt thou part from me!
His lips to mine, to mine, all trembling, pressed.
The writer was our Galeot with his book: —
That day we read no further on." She stopped:
Meanwhile he moaned so that compassion took
My sense away, and like a corse I dropped.

Observe that Dr. Parsons has put Dante's twenty-eight lines of eleven syllables into twenty-four lines of ten syllables; and this without losing a drop of the precious stream he undertakes to pour. But why does he make Francesca address her companion personally, instead of saying, "who shall never part from me?" And why does Mr. Dayman say, "pious drops," instead of piteous? Mr. Dayman and Mr. Longfellow fill up the twenty-eight lines. In neither of the three is there any strain or wresting of the sense. But all three, and before them Lord Byron and Carey, mistranslate this passage,—

> "Per piu fiate gli occhi ci sospinse
> Quella lettura."

All these translators interpret it to mean, that while they read, their eyes often met; whereas Dante says, they read that passage over more than once; or, literally rendered, several times that reading or passage drew to it their eyes. To restore the meaning of the original adds to the refinement of the scene.

Why does Mr. Longfellow use such long words as *compassionate* instead of *pitiful* or *piteous, recognize* for *know, palpitating* for *trembling, conceded that you should know* for *gave you to know?* By the resolution to translate line for line, Mr. Longfellow ties his poetic hands. The first effect of this self-binding is, to oblige him to use often long Latin-English instead of short Saxon-English words, that is, words that in most cases lend themselves less readily to poetic expression. Mr. Dayman, not translating line for line, is free from this prosaic incumbrance; but as he makes it a rule to himself that every English canto shall contain the same number of lines as its original, he is obliged, much more often than Mr. Longfellow, to throw in epithets or words not in the Italian. And Dr. Parsons, who, happily freeing himself from either verbal or numerical bond, in several instances compresses a canto into two or three lines less than the Italian, and the XXXI. into nine lines less, might with advantage have curtailed each canto ten or twelve lines.

Do what we will, poetic translation is brought about more from without than from within, and hence there is apt to be a dryness of surface, a lack of that sheen, that spontaneous warm emanation, which, in good original work, comes from free inward impulsion. To counteract, in so far as may be, this proneness to a mechanical inflexibility, the translator should keep himself free to wield boldly and with full swing his own native speech. By his line-for-line allegiance, Mr. Longfellow forfeits much of this freedom. He is too intent on the words; he sacrifices the spirit to the letter; he overlays the poetry with a verbal literalness; he deprives himself of scope to give a billowy motion, a heightened color, a girded vigor, to choice passages. The rhythmical languor consequent on this verbal conformity, this lineal servility, is increased by a frequent looseness in the endings of lines, some of which on every page, and many on some pages, have — contrary to all good usage — the superfluous eleventh syllable. Milton never allows himself this liberty, nor Mr. Tennyson in epic verse so little pretentious as "Idyls of the King." Nor do good blank-verse translators give in to it. Cowper does not in his Iliad, nor Lord Derby, nor Mr. Bryant in his version of the fifth book of the Odyssey, nor Mr. Carey in his Dante. Permissible at times in dramatic blank verse, it is in epic rejected by the best artists as a weakness. Can it be that Mr. Longfellow hereby aims to be more close to the form of Dante? Whatever the cause of its use, the effect is still farther to weaken his translation. These loose poetic endings — and on most pages one third of the lines have eleven syllables and on some pages more than a third — do a part in causing Mr. Longfellow's Dante to lack the clean outline, the tonic ring, the chiseled edge of the original, and in making his cantos read as would sound a high passionate tune played on a harp whose strings are relaxed.

Looking at the printed Italian Dante beside the English, in a volume where opposite each

English page is the corresponding page of the original, as in Mr. Dayman's, one cannot fail to be struck with the comparative narrowness of the Italian column. This comes of the comparative shortness of Italian syllables. For instance, as the strongest exemplification, the ever-recurring *and,* and the often-repeated *is,* are both expressed in Italian by a single letter, *e.* And this shortness comes of the numerousness of vowels. In lines of thirty letters Dante will have on an average sixteen consonants to fourteen vowels, nearly half and half; while his translators have about twenty consonants to ten vowels, or two to one. From this comparative rejection of consonants, Italian cannot, as English can, bind into one syllable words of seven or eight letters, like *friends* and *straight,* nor even words of six letters, like *chimed, shoots, thwart, spring;* nor does Italian abound as English does in monosyllables, and the few it has are mostly of but two or three letters. In combination its syllables sometimes get to four letters, as in *fronte* and *braccia.* As a consequence hereof, Dante's lines, although always of eleven syllables, average about twenty-nine letters, while those of the three translators about thirty-three. Hence, the poem in their versions carries more weight than the original; its soul is more cumbered with body.

In order to the faithful reproduction of Dante, to the giving the best transcript, possible in English, of his thought and feeling, should not regard be had to the essential difference between the syllabic constitutions of the two languages, what may be called the physical basis of the two mediums of utterance? Here is the Francesca story, translated in the spirit of this suggestion:—

I turned to them, and then I spake:
  "Francesca! tears o'erfill mine eyes,
Such pity thy keen pangs awake.
  But say: in th' hour of sweetest sighs,
By what and how found Love relief
  And broke thy doubtful longing's spell?"
And she: "There is no greater grief
  Than joy in sorrow to retell.
But if so urgently one seeks
  To know our Love's first root, I will
Do as he does who weeps and speaks.
  One day of Lancelot we still
Read o'er, how love held him enchained.
  Without mistrust we were alone.
Our cheeks oft were of color drained:
  One passage vanquished us, but one.
When we read of lips longed for pressed
  By such a lover with a kiss,
This one whom naught from me shall wrest,
  All trembling kissed my mouth. To this

That book and writer brought us. We
  No farther read that day." While she
Thus spake, the other spirit wept
  So bitterly, with pity I
Fell motionless, my senses swept
  By swoon, as one about to die.

In the very first line two Italian trisyllables, *rivolsi* and *parlai*, are given in English with literal fidelity by two monosyllables, *turned* and *spake*. In the fourth observe how, in a word-for-word rendering, the eleven Italian syllables become, without any forcing, eight English:

"Ma dimmi: al tempo de' dolci sospiri:"
"But tell me: in th' hour of sweet sighs."

For the sake of a more musical cadence, this line is slightly modified. Again, in the line,—

"Than joy in sorrow to retell,"

joy represents, and represents faithfully, three words containing six syllables, *del tempo felice: retell* stands for *ricordarsi*, and *in sorrow* for *nella miseria*, or, three syllables for six; so that, by means of eight syllables, is given a full and complete translation of what in Italian takes up seventeen. English the most simple, direct, idiomatic, is needed in order that a translation of Dante be faithful to his simplicity and naturalness; and this is the first fidelity his translator should feel himself bound to. Owing to the fundamental difference between the syllabic structures of the two languages, we are enabled to put into English lines of eight syllables the whole meaning of Dante's lines of eleven. In the above experiment even more has been done. The twenty-eight lines of Dante are given in twenty-six lines of eight syllables each, and this without any sacrifice of the thought or feeling; for the "this thy teacher knows," which is omitted, besides that the commentators cannot agree on its meaning, is parenthetical in sense, and with reverence be it said, in so far a defect in such a relation. As to the form of Dante, what is essential in that has been preserved, namely, the iambic measure and the rhyme.

Let us try if this curtailment of syllables will be successful when applied to the terrible words, written in blackest color, over the gate of Hell, at the beginning of the third canto of the "Inferno":—

Through me the path to place of wail:
  Through me the path to endless sigh:
Through me the path to souls in bale.
  'Twas Justice moved my Maker high:
Wisdom supreme, and Might divine,
  And primal Love established me.
Created birth was none ere mine,
  And I endure eternally:
Ye who pass in, all hope resign.

Has anything been lost in the transit from Italian words to English? English speech being organically more concentrated than Italian, does not the reduction of eleven syllables to eight especially subserve what ought to be the twofold aim of all poetic translation, namely, along with fidelity to the thought and spirit of the original, fidelity to the idiom, and cast and play of the translator's own tongue?

Here is another short passage in a different key, — the opening of the last canto of the "Paradiso": —

> Maid-mother, daughter of thy Son,
> Meek, yet above all things create,
> Fair aim of the Eternal one,
> 'Tis thou who so our human state
> Ennobledst, that its Maker deigned
> Himself his creature's son to be.
> This flower, in th' endless peace, was gained
> Through kindling of God's love in thee.

In this passage nine Italian lines of eleven syllables are converted into eight lines of eight syllables each. We submit it to the candid reader of Italian to say, whether aught of the original has been sacrificed to brevity.

The rejection of all superfluity, the conciseness and simplicity to which the translator is obliged by octosyllabic verse, compensate for the partial loss of that breadth of sweep for which decasyllabic verse gives more room, but of which the translator of Dante does not feel the want.

One more short passage of four lines, — the famous figure of the lark in the twentieth Canto of the "Paradiso": —

Like lark that through the air careers,
  First singing, then, silent his heart,
Feeds on the sweetness in his ears,
  Such joy to th' image did impart
Th' eternal will.

This paper has exceeded the length we designed to give it; but, nevertheless, we beg the reader's indulgence for a few moments longer, while we conclude with an octosyllabic version of the last thirty lines of the celebrated Ugolino story. It is unrhymed; for that terrible tale can dispense, in English, with soft echoes at the end of lines.

When locked I heard the nether door
Of the dread tower, I without speech
Into my children's faces looked:
Nor wept, so inly turned to stone.
They wept: and my dear Anselm said,
"Thou look'st so, father, what hast thou?"
Still I nor wept nor answer made
That whole day through, nor the next night,
Till a new sun rose on the world.

As in our doleful prison came
A little glimmer, and I saw
On faces four my own pale stare,
Both of my hands for grief I bit;
And they, thinking it was from wish
To eat, rose suddenly and said:
'Father, less shall we feel of pain
If thou wilt eat of us: from thee
Came this poor flesh: take it again."
I calmed me then, not to grieve them.
The next two days we spake no word.
Oh! obdurate earth, why didst not ope?
When we had come to the fourth day
Gaddo threw him stretched at my feet,
Saying, "Father, why dost not help me?"
There died he; and, as thou seest me,
I saw the three fall one by one
The fifth and sixth day; then I groped,
Now blind, o'er each; and two whole days
I called them after they were dead:
Then hunger did what grief could not.

V.

SAINTE-BEUVE, THE CRITIC.

A LITERARY critic, a genuine one, should carry in his brain an arsenal of opposites. He should combine common sense with tact, integrity with indulgence, breadth with keenness, vigor with delicacy, largeness with subtlety, knowledge with geniality, inflexibility with sinuousness, severity with suavity; and, that all these counter qualities be effective, he will need constant culture and vigilance, besides the union of reason with warmth, of enthusiasm with self-control, of wit with philosophy, — but hold: at this rate, in order to fit out the critic, human nature will have to set apart its highest and best. Dr. Johnson declared, the poet ought to know everything and to have seen everything, and the ancients required the like of an orator. Truly, the supreme poet should have manifold gifts, be humanly indued as generously and completely as is the bust of Homer, ideally shaped by the light of the infallible artistic instinct and insight of the Greeks. The poet, it is true, must be born a poet, and the critic is the child of culture. But as the poet, to perfect his birthright, has need of culture, so the man whom culture can shape and sharpen to the good critic, must be born with many gifts, to be susceptible of such shaping. And when we reflect that the task of the critic is to see clearly into the subtlest and deepest mind, to measure its hollows and its elevations, to weigh all its individual and its composite powers, and, that from every one of the throbbing aggregates, whom it is his office to analyze and portray, issue lines that run on all sides into the infinite, we must conclude that he who is to be the accomplished interpreter, the trusted judge, should be able swiftly to follow these lines.

Long and exacting as is our roll of what is wanted to equip a veritable sure critic, we have yet to add two cardinal qualifications, which by the subject of our present paper are possessed in liberal allotment. The first is, joy in life, from which the pages of M. Sainte-Beuve derive, not a superficial sprightliness merely, but a mellow, radiant geniality. The other, which is of still deeper account, is the capacity of admiration ; a virtue — for so it deserves to be called — born directly of the nobler sensibilities, those in whose presence only can be recognized and enjoyed the lofty and the profound, the beautiful and the true. He who is not well endowed with these higher senses is not a bad critic; he is no critic at all. Not only can he not discern the good there is in a man or a work, he can as little discover and expose the bad; for, deficiencies implying failures to reach a certain fullness, implying a falling short of the complete, to say where and what are deficiencies, involves the having in the mind an idea of the full and complete. The man so meagrely furnished as to hold no such idea is but a carper, not a critic. To know the bad denotes knowledge of the good; in criticism as in morals, a righteous indignation can only flash from a shock to pure feelings.

In a notice of M. Thiers' chapter on St. Helena, M. Sainte-Beuve, after expressing his admiration of the commentaries of Napoleon on the campaigns of Turenne, Frederic, and Cæsar, adds: "A man of letters smiles at first involuntarily to see Napoleon apply to each of these famous campaigns a methodical criticism, just as we would proceed with a work of the mind, with an epic or tragic poem. But is not a campaign of a great captain equally a work of genius? Napoleon is here the high sovereign critic, the Goethe in this department, as the Feuquières, the Jominis, the St. Cyrs are the La Harpes or the Fontanes, the Lessings or the Schlegels, all good and expert critics; but he is the first of all, nor, if you reflect on it, could it have been otherwise. And who then would say better things of Homer than Milton?" — Goethe supreme in literary criticism, Milton on Homer; this touches the root of the matter; sympathy with the writer and his work the critic must have, — sympathy as one of the sources of good judgment, and even of knowledge. You cannot know, and therefore not judge of a man or book or thing, unless you have some fellow-feeling with him or it; and to judge well you must have much fellow-feeling. The critic must, moreover, be a thinker; reason is the critic's sun. Scott and Byron could say just and fresh things about poets and poetry; but neither could command the whole field, nor dig deep into the soil. Witness Byron's deliberate exaltation of Pope. Whereas Wordsworth and Coleridge were among the soundest of critics, because, besides being poets, they were both profound thinkers.

For the perfecting of the literary critic the especial sympathy needed is that with excellence; for high literature is the outcome of the best there is in humanity, the finished expression of healthiest aspirations, of choicest thoughts, the ripened fruit of noble, of refined growths, the perfected fruit, with all the perfume and beauty of the flower upon it. Of this sympathy M. Sainte-Beuve, throughout his many volumes, gives overflowing evidence, in addition to that primary proof of having himself written good poems. Besides the love, he has the instinct, of literature, and this instinct draws him to what is its bloom and fullest manifestation, and his love is the more warm and constant for being discriminative and refined. Through variety of knowledge, with intellectual keenness, he enjoys excellence in the diversified forms that literature assumes. His pages abound in illustrations of his versatility, which is nowhere more strikingly exhibited than in the contrast between two successive papers (both equally admirable) in the very first volume of the "Causeries du Lundi," the one on Madame Récamier, the other on Napoleon. Read especially the series of paragraphs beginning, "Some natures are born pure, and have received *quand même* the gift of innocence," to see how gracefully, subtly, delicately, with what a feminine tenderness, he draws the portrait of this most fascinating of women, this beautiful creature, for whom grace and sweetness did even still more than beauty, this fairy-queen of France, this refined coquette, who drew to her hundreds of hearts, this kindly magician, who turned all her lovers into friends. Then pass directly to the next paper, on the terrible Corsican, "who weakened his greatness by the gigantic — who loved to astonish — who delighted too much in what was his forte, war, — who was too much a bold adventurer." And further on, the account of Napoleon's conversation with Goethe at Weimar, in which account M. Sainte-Beuve shows how fully he values the largeness and truthfulness and penetration of the great German. The impression thus made on the reader as to the variousness of M. Sainte-Beuve's power is deepened by another paper in the same volume, that on M. Guizot and his historic school, a masterly paper, which reasons convincingly against those historians who strain humanity, who make the lesson that history teaches too direct and stiff, who put themselves in the place of Providence," which, as is said in another place (vol. v. p. 150), "is often but a deification of our own thought."

In a paper published in 1862, M. Sainte-Beuve—who had then, for more than thirty years, been plying zealously and continuously the function of critic—describes what is a fundamental feature of his method in arriving at a judgment on books and authors. "Literature, literary production, is in my eyes not distinct, or at least not separable, from the rest of the man and his organization. I can enjoy a work, but it is difficult for me to form a judgment on it independently of the man himself; and I readily say, *as is the tree so is the fruit.* Literary study thus leads me quite naturally to moral study." This, of course, he can apply but partially to the ancients; but with the moderns the first thing to do in order to know the work is to know the man who did it, to get at his primary organization, his interior beginnings and proclivities; and to learn this, one of the best means is, to make yourself acquainted with his race, his family, his predecessors. "You are sure to recognize the superior man, in part at least, in his parents, especially in his mother, the most direct and certain of his parents ; also in his sisters and his brothers, even in his children. In these one discovers important features which, from being too condensed, too closely joined in the eminent individual, are masked ; but whereof the basis, the *fond,* is found in others of his blood in a more naked, a more simple state."

Hereby is shown with what thoroughness and professional conscientiousness M. Sainte-Beuve sets himself to his work of critic. Partially applying to himself his method, we discover in part the cause of his sympathy for feminine nature, and of his tact in delineating it. His father died before he was born ; and thence all living parental influence on him was maternal. None of his volumes is more captivating than his "Portraits de Femmes," a translation of which we are glad to see announced.

Of Sainte-Beuve's love for excellence there is, in the third volume of the "Nouveaux Lundis," an illustration, eloquently disclosing how deep is his sympathy with the most excellent that human kind has known. For the London Exposition of 1862 a magnificent folio of the New Testament was prepared at the Imperial Press of Paris. The critic takes the occasion to write a paper on "Les saints Evangiles," especially the Sermon on the Mount. After quoting and commenting on the Beatitudes, he continues: "Had there ever before been heard in the world such accents, such a love of poverty, of self-divestment, such a hunger and thirst for justice, such eagerness to suffer for it, to be cursed of men in behalf of it, such an intrepid confidence in celestial recompense, such a forgiveness of injuries, and not simply forgiveness but a livelier feeling of charity for those who have injured you, who persecute and calumniate you, such a form of prayer and of familiar address to the Father who is in heaven? Was there ever before anything like to that, so encouraging, so consoling, in the teaching and the precepts of the sages? Was that not truly a revelation in the midst of human morals; and if there be joined to it, what cannot be separated from it, the totality of such a life, spent in doing good, and that predication of about three years, crowned by the crucifixion, have we not a right to say that here was a 'new ideal of a soul perfectly heroic,' which, under this half Jewish, Galilean form was set before all coming generations?

"Who talks to us of *myth*, of the realization, more or less instinctive or philosophical, of the human conscience reflecting itself in a being who only supplied the pretext and who hardly existed. What! do you not feel the reality, the living, vibrating, bleeding, compassionate personality, which, independently of what belief and enthusiasm may have added, exists and throbs behind such words? What more convincing demonstration of the beauty and truth of the entirely historic personage, Jesus, than the Sermon on the Mount?"

Alluding, then, to the denial of originality in the moral doctrines of Christianity, M. Sainte-Beuve, after citing from Socrates, Marcus Aurelius, and others, passages wherein is recommended "charity toward the human race," declares that all these examples and precepts, all that makes a fine body of social and philosophical morality, is not Christianity itself as beheld at its source and in its spirit. "What characterizes," he proceeds, "the discourse on the mount and the other sayings and parables of Jesus, is not the charity that relates to equity and strict justice, to which, with a sound heart and upright spirit, one attains; it is something unknown to flesh and blood and to simple reason, it is a kind of innocent and pure exaltation, freed from rule and superior to law, holily improvident, a stranger to all calculation, to all positive prevision, unreservedly reliant on Him who sees and knows all things, and as a last reward counting on the coming of that kingdom of God, the promise of which cannot fail:—

But I say unto you, That ye resist not evil: but whosoever shall smite thee on thy right cheek, turn to him the other also.

And if any man will sue thee at the law, and take away thy coat, let him have thy cloak also. . . . .

Give to him that asketh thee, and from him that would borrow of thee turn not thou away. . . . .

No man can serve two masters: for either he will hate the one, and love the other; or else he will hold to the one, and despise the other. Ye cannot serve God and mammon.

Therefore I say unto you, Take no thought for your life, what ye shall eat, or what ye shall drink; nor yet for your body, what ye shall put on. Is not the life more than meat, and the body than raiment? . . . .

"Nothing of this is to be found in the ancient sages and moralists, not in Hesiod, nor in the maxims of Greece any more than in Confucius. It is not in Cicero, nor in Aristotle, nor even in Socrates any more than in the modern Franklin. The principle of inspiration is different, if indeed it be not opposite: the paths may come together for a moment, but they cross one another. And it is this delicate ideal of devotedness, of moral purification, of continual renouncement and self-sacrifice, breathing in the words and embodied in the person and life of Christ, which constitutes the entire novelty as well as the sublimity of Christianity taken at its source."

Of M. Sainte-Beuve's delight in what is the most excellent product of literature, poetry, testimony is borne by many papers, ranging over the whole field of French poetry, from its birth to its latest page. "Poetry," says he, "is the essence of things, and we should be careful not to spread the drop of essence through a mass of water or floods of color. The task of poetry is not to say everything, but to make us dream everything." And he cites a similar judgment of Fénélon: "The poet should take only the flower of each object, and never touch but what can be beautified." In a critique of Alfred de Musset he speaks of the youthful poems of Milton: "'Il Penseroso' is the masterpiece of meditative and contemplative poetry; it is like a magnificent oratorio in which prayer ascends slowly toward the Eternal. I make no comparison; let us never take august names from their sphere. All that is beautiful in Milton stands by itself; one feels the tranquil habit of the upper regions, and continuity in power." In a paper on the letters of Ducis, he proves that he apprehends the proportions of Shakespeare. He asks: "Have we then got him at last? Is our stomach up to him? Are we strong enough to digest this marrow of lion (*cette moelle de lion*)?" And again, in an article on the men of the eighteenth century, he writes: "One may be born a sailor, but there is nothing for it like seeing a storm, nor for a soldier like seeing a battle. A Shakespeare, you will say, very nearly did without all that, and yet he knew it all. But Nature never but once made a Shakespeare."

Like most writers, of whatever country, M. Sainte-Beuve has formed himself on native models, and the French having no poet of the highest class, no Dante, no Shakespeare, no Goethe, it is a further proof of his breadth and insight that he should so highly value the treasures in the deeper mines opened by these foreigners. Seeing, too, how catholic he is, and liberal toward all other greatness, one even takes pleasure in his occasional exuberance of national complacency. Whenever he speaks of Montaigne or La Fontaine or Molière, his words flame with a tempered enthusiasm. But he throws no dust in his own eyes: his is a healthy rapture, a torch lighted by the feelings, but which the reason holds upright and steady. His native favorites he enjoys as no Englishman or German could, but he does not overrate them. Nor does he overrate Voltaire, whom he calls "the Frenchman par excellence," and of whom he is proud as the literary sovereign of his age. At the same time, in articles directly devoted to Joubert, as well as by frequent citations of his judgments, he lauds this spiritually-minded thinker as one of the best of critics. And yet of Voltaire, Joubert says the hardest things: "Voltaire is sometimes sad; he is excited; but he is never serious. His graces even are impudent. — There are defects difficult to perceive, that have not been classed or defined, and have no names. Voltaire is full of them."

In a paper on Louise Labé, a poetess of the sixteenth century, he reproduces some of her poems and several passages of prose, and then adds: "These passages prove, once more, the marked superiority that, at almost all times, French prose has over French poetry." No German or English or Italian critic could say this of his native literature, and the saying of it by the foremost of French critics is not an exaltation of French prose, it is a depression of French poetry. In this judgment there is a reach and severity of which possibly the eminent critic was not fully conscious ; for it amounts to an acknowledgment that the nature and language of the French are not capable of producing and embodying the highest poetry.

Goethe, M. Sainte-Beuve always mentions with deference. On Eckerman's "Conversations with Goethe" he has a series of three papers, wherein he deals chiefly with the critic and sage, exhibiting with honest pride Goethe's admiration of some of the chief French writers, and his acknowledgment of what he owed them. To a passage relating to the French translation of Eckerman, M. Sainte-Beuve has the following note, which we, on this side the Atlantic, may cherish as a high tribute to our distinguished countrywoman : "The English translation is by Miss Fuller, afterwards Marchioness Ossoli, who perished so unhappily by shipwreck. An excellent preface precedes this translation, and I must say that for elevated comprehension of the subject and for justness of appreciation it leaves our preface far behind it. Miss Fuller, an American lady of Boston, was a person of true merit and of great intellectual vigor." A sympathetic student of Goethe, Margaret Fuller purposed to write a life of him; and seeing what critical capacity and what insight into the nature of Goethe she has shown in this preface, we may be confident that she would have made a genuine contribution to the Goethe "literature," had she lived to do that and other high literary work. Her many friends had nearer and warmer motives for deploring the early loss of this gifted, generous, noble-hearted woman.

One of the busiest functions of the critic being to sift the multifarious harvest of contemporaneous literature, he must have a hand that can shake hard, — and hit hard, too, at times. For fifteen years M. Sainte-Beuve furnished once a week, under the title of "Causeries du Lundi," a critical paper, to a Paris daily journal; not short, rapid notices, but articles that would cover seven or eight pages of one of our double-columned monthly magazines. He was thus ever in the thick of the literary *mêlée*. Attractions and repulsions, sympathies and antipathies, there will be wherever men do congregate; the æsthetic plane is as open as any other to personal preferences and friendships.

A literary circle as large as that of Paris, if too miscellaneous and extensive to become one multitudinous mutual-admiration-society, will, through cliques and coteries, betray some of its vices. In this voluminous series of papers the critical pen, when most earnestly eulogistic or most sharply incisive, is wielded with so much skill and art and fine temper, that personality is seldom transpicuous. The Parisian reader will no doubt often perceive, in this or that paragraph or paper, a heightening or a subduing of color not visible to the foreigner, who cannot so well trace the marks of political, religious, or personal influences. His perfected praise M. Sainte-Beuve reserves for those of the illustrious dead who are embalmed in their own excellence. Besides devoting many papers (among the most valuable of the series) to these magnates of literature, he delights in frequent illustrative reference to them, — a sign this of ripe culture in a critic, and of trustworthiness.

Out of the severe things occasionally said, the sting is mostly taken by the temper in which they are said, or by the frank recognition of virtues and beauties beside vices and blemishes. In the general tone there is a clear humanity, a seemly gentlemanliness. Of the humane spirit wherewith M. Sainte-Beuve tempers condemnation, take the following as one of many instances. In the correspondence of Lamennais there is laid bare such contradictions between his earlier and his later sentiments on religious questions, that the reader is thus feelingly guarded against being too harsh in his censure: "Let us cast a look on ourselves, and ask if in our lives, in our hearts, from youth to our latter years, there are none of these boundless distances, these secret abysses, these moral ruins, perhaps, which, for being hidden, are none the less real and profound."

Writing weekly for the *feuilleton* of a Paris daily journal, M. Sainte-Beuve cannot but be sometimes diffuse; but his diffuseness is always animated, never languid. Fluent, conversational, ever polished, he is full of happy turns and of Gallic sprightliness. When the occasion offers, he is concise, condensed even in the utterance of a principle or of a comprehensive thought. "Admiration is a much finer test of literary talent, a sign much more sure and delicate, than all the art of satire." By the side of this may be placed a sentence he cites from Grimm: "People who so easily admire bad things are not in a state to enjoy good." How true and cheering is this: "There is in each of us a primitive ideal being, whom Nature has wrought with her finest and most maternal hand, but whom man too often covers up, smothers, or corrupts." Speaking of the sixteenth century, he says: "What it wanted was taste, if by taste we understand choice clean and perfect, the disengagement of the elements of the beautiful." When, to give a paragraph its fit ending, the thought allows of an epigrammatic point, if he does not happen to have one of his own he knows where to borrow just what is wanted. Speaking of embellished oratorical diction, he quotes Talleyrand on some polished oration that was discussed in his presence: "It is not enough to have fine sentences: you must have something to put into them." Commenting on the hyper-spirituality of M. Laprade, he says: "M. Laprade starts from the *absolute notion of being*. For him the following is the principle of Art, — 'to manifest what we feel of the Absolute Being, of the Infinite, of God, to make him known and felt by other men, such in its generality is the end of Art.' Is this true, is it false? I know not: at this elevation one always gets into the clouds. Like the most of those who pride themselves on metaphysics, he contents himself with words (*il se paye de mots*)." Here is a grand thought, that flashes out of the upper air of poetry: "Humanity, that eternal child that has never done growing."

M. Sainte-Beuve's irony, keen and delicate, is a sprightly medium of truth: witness this passage on a new volume of M. Michelet: "Narrative, properly so called, which never was his forte, is almost entirely sacrificed. Seek here no historical highway, well laid, solid, and continuous; the method adopted is absolute points of view; you run with him on summits, peaks, on needles of granite, which he selects at his pleasure to gets views from. The reader leaps from steeple to steeple. M. Michelet seems to have proposed to himself an impossible wager, which, however, he has won, — to write history with a series of flashes." Could there be a more subtle, covert way of saying of a man that he is hardened by self-esteem than the following on M. Guizot: "The consciousness that he has of himself, and a natural principle of pride, place him easily above the little susceptibilities of self-love." M. Sainte-Beuve is not an admirer of Louis Philippe, and among other sly hits gives him the following: "Louis Philippe was too much like a *bourgeois* himself to be long respected by the *bourgeoisie*. Just as in former times the King of France was only the first gentleman of the kingdom, he was nothing but the first *bourgeois* of the country." What witty satire on Lamartine he introduces, with a recognition of popularity that, with one who takes so much joy in applause as Lamartine does, is enough to take the poison out of the sting: "Those who knew his verses by heart (and the number who do is large among the men of our age) meet, not without regret, with whole strips of them spread out, drowned, as it were, in his prose. This prose is, in 'Les Confidences,' too often but the paraphrase of his verses, which were themselves become, toward the last, paraphrases of his feelings." Amends are made to Lamartine on another occasion, when, citing some recent French sonnets, he says: "Neither Lamartine nor Hugo nor Vigny wrote sonnets. The swans and the eagles, in trying to enter this cage, would have broken their wings. That was for us, birds of a less lofty flight and less amplitude of wing." This is better as modesty than as criticism. Shakespeare, Milton, Wordsworth, had wings of vaster sweep as well as of more gorgeous plumage than these French soarers, and they enjoyed getting into the cage of the sonnet, and sang therein some of their strongest as well as sweetest notes.

A thorough Frenchman, M. Sainte-Beuve delights in French minds, just as a beauty delights in her mirror, which throws back an image of herself. His excellence as a critic is primarily owing to this joy in things French. Through means of it he knows them through and through: they are become transparent; and while his feelings are aglow, his intellect looks calmly right through them, and sees on the other side the shadows cast by the spots and opacities which frustrate more or less the fullest illumination. Freely he exhibits these shadows. Neither Bossuet nor Louis XIV., neither Voltaire nor Béranger, is spared, nor the French character, with its proneness to frivolity and broad jest, its thirst for superficial excitement. Whatever his individual preferences, his mental organization is so large and happy, that he enjoys, and can do equal justice to, Father Lacordaire and M. Michelet, to Madame de Staël and M. Guizot, to Corneille and Goethe, to Fénélon and M. Renan, to Marie Antoinette and Mirabeau.

Have you then for M. Sainte-Beuve, some reader will be impatient to ask, nothing but praise? Not much else. Commencing his literary career in 1827, when only in his twenty-third year, from that date to 1849 his writings, chiefly in the shape of literary portraits, fill several thousand pages. Between his forty-fifth to his sixtieth year he wrote twenty-three volumes, containing about eleven thousand pages, on four or five hundred different authors and subjects. This is the period of his critical maturity, the period of the "Causeries du Lundi," followed by the "Nouveaux Lundis." Many men write voluminously, but most of these only write *about* a subject, not *into* it. Only the few who can write into their subject add something to literature. One of these few is M. Sainte-Beuve. In his mind there is vitality to animate his large acquirement, to make his many chapters buoyant and stimulant. All through his writings is the sparkle of original life.

But let us now cheer the reader who is impatient of much praise, and at the same time perform the negative part of our task.

Well, then, to be bold, as befits a critic of the critic, we beard the lion in his very den. We challenge a definition he gives of the critic. In the seventh volume of the "Causeries," article "Grimm," he says: "When Nature has endowed some one with this vivacity of feeling, with this susceptibility to impression, and that the creative imagination be wanting, this some one is a born critic, that is to say, a lover and judge of the creations of others." Why did M. Sainte-Beuve make Goethe sovereign in criticism? Why did he think Milton peculiarly qualified to interpret Homer? From the deep principle of like unto like; only spirit can know spirit. What were the worth of a comment of John Locke on "Paradise Lost," except to reveal the mental composition of John Locke? The critic should be what Locke was, a thinker, but to be a judge of the highest form of literature, poetry, he must moreover carry within him, inborn, some share of that whereby poetry is fledged, "creative imagination." He may "want the accomplishment of verse," or the constructive faculty, but more than the common allowance of sensibility to the beautiful he must have. But do not the presence of "vivacity of feeling with susceptibility to impression" imply the imaginative temperament? If not, then we confidently assure M. Sainte-Beuve that had his definition fitted himself, his "Causeries du Lundi" would never have been rescued from the quick oblivion of the *feuilleton.*

Now and then there are betrayals of that predominant French weakness, which the French will persist in cherishing as a virtue, — the love of glory. M. Sainte-Beuve thinks Buffon's passion for glory saved him in his latter years from ennui, from "that languor of the soul which follows the age of the passions." Where are to be found men more the victims of disgust with life than that eminent pair, not more distinguished for literary brilliancy and contemporaneous success than for insatiable greed of glory, — Byron and Chateaubriand? No form of self-seeking is morally more weakening than this quenchless craving, which makes the soul hang its satisfaction on what is utterly beyond its sway, on praise and admiration. These stimulants — withdrawn more or less even from the most successful in latter years — leave a void which becomes the very nursery of ennui, or even of self-disgust. Instead of glory being "the potent motive-power in all great souls," as M. Sainte-Beuve approvingly quotes, it is, with a surer moral instinct, called by Milton, —

> "That last infirmity of noble mind."

In some of the noblest and greatest, so subordinate is it as hardly to be traceable in their careers. Love of glory was not the spring that set and kept in motion Kepler and Newton, any more than Shakespeare and Pascal or William of Orange and Washington.

The military glory wherewith Napoleon fed and flattered the French nation for fifteen years, and the astonishing intellectual and animal vigor of the conqueror's mind, dazzle even M. Sainte-Beuve, so that he does not perceive the gaping chasms in Napoleon's moral nature, and the consequent one-sidedness of his intellectual action, nor the unmanning effects of his despotism. The words used to describe the moral side of the Imperial career are as insufficient as would be the strokes of a gray crayon to depict a conflagration or a sunset. In the paper from which has already been quoted he speaks of the "rare good sense" of Napoleon, of "his instinct of justice." But was it not a compact array of the selfish impulses against a weak instinct of justice, backed by a Titan's will, wielding a mighty intellect, that enabled Napoleon to be the disloyal usurper, then the hardened despot and the merciless devastator? Again, can it be said of Napoleon that he possessed good sense in a rare degree? Good sense is an instinctive insight into all the bearings of act or thought, an intuitive discernment of the relations and consequences of conduct or purpose, a soundness of judgment, resulting from the soundness of, and equilibrium among, the upper powers of reason and sensibility. The moral side is at least the half of it: Napoleon's moral endowment was but fractional. Good sense, it may be added, lies solidly at the basis of all good work, except such as is purely professional or technical, or in its action one-sided; and even in such its presence must be felt. In whatever reaches general human interests, whether as practical act or imaginative creation, good sense must be, for their prosperity, a primary ingredient. "The Tempest" and "Don Quixote" shoot up into shining, imperishable beauty because their roots draw their first nourishment from this hearty, inexhaustible substratum. And let us say, that in M. Sainte-Beuve himself good sense is the foundation of his eminent critical ability. He has been led, we conceive, to attribute more of it to Napoleon than is his due by the blinding splendor of Napoleon's military genius, through which, with such swiftness and cumulative effect, he adapted means to ends on the purely material plane.

When Murray applied to Lord Byron to write a book about the life and manners of the upper class in Italy, Byron declined the proposal from personal regards, and then added, that were he to write such a book it would be misjudged in England; for, said he, "their moral is not your moral." Such international misinterpretations and exaggerations are instinctive and involuntary. A nation from its being a nation, has a certain one-sidedness. To the Italian (even to one who carries a stiletto) the English practice of boxing is a sheer brutality; while to an Englishman (himself perhaps not a Joseph) the *cavaliere servente* is looked upon with reprobation tempered by scorn. To this misjudgment from the foreign side and over-estimation on the domestic, books, too, are liable; but to books as being more abstract than usages, more ideal than manners, an absolute moral standard can with less difficulty be applied. Applying it to Gil Blas, is not M. Sainte-Beuve subject to arraignment when he speaks of this and the other writings of Le Sage as being "the mirror of the world?" Molière, too, is a satirist, and from his breadth a great one; and surely the world he holds a mirror before is a much purer world than that of Le Sage; and what of the Shakespearean world? The world of Le Sage is a nether world. "Of Gil Blas it has been well said that the book is moral like experience." The experience one may get in brothels and "hells," in consorting with pimps and knaves, has in it lessons of virtue and morality,—for those who can extract them; but even for these few it is a very partial teaching; and for the many who cannot read so spiritually, whether in the book or the brothel, the experience is demoralizing and deadening. But toward the end of the paper the critic lets it appear that he does not place Le Sage so high as some of his phrases prompt us to infer; and he quotes this judgment of Joubert: "Of the novels of Le Sage it may be said that they seem to have been written in a *café*, by a player of dominoes, on coming out of the comic theatre."

Without being over-diffident, we may feel our footing not perfectly secure on French ground when we differ from a Frenchman; we are therefore not sorry to catch M. Sainte-Beuve tripping on English ground. In a review of the translation of the celebrated Letters of Lord Chesterfield—whom he calls the La Rochefoucauld of England—he refers to, and in part quotes, the passages in which Chesterfield gives his son advice as to his *liaisons;* and he adds: "All Chesterfield's morality, on this head, is resumed in a line of Voltaire, —

"Il n'est jamais de mal en bonne compagnie."

It is these passages that make the grave Dr. Johnson blush: we only smile at them." For ourselves, we blush with Johnson, not that the man of the world should give to his youthful son, living at a corrupt Continental court, counsel as to relations which were regarded as inevitable in such a circle; but that the heart of the father should not have poured (were it but parenthetically) through the pen of the worldling some single sentence like this: "Writing to you, my son, as an experienced man of the world to one inexperienced, I recommend the good taste in such matters and the delicacy which become a gentleman; but to his dear boy, your father says, avoid, if possible, such *liaisons;* preserve your purity; nothing will give you such a return throughout the whole of the future." But, a single sentence like this would *vitiate* the entire Chesterfieldian correspondence.

How fully and warmly M. Sainte-Beuve prizes moral worth may be learnt from many passages.

Not the least animated and cordial of his papers is one on the Abbé Gerbet, in the sixth volume, a paper which shows, as Gustave Planche said of him, that "he studies with his heart, as women do;" and one in the second volume on Malesherbes, whom he describes as being "separated, on the moral side, from the Mirabeaus and the Condorcets not by a shade, but by an abyss," and whom he sums up as "great magistrate, minister too sensitive and too easily discouraged, heroic advocate, and sublime victim." Of this noble, deeply dutiful, self-sacrificing Frenchman, this exemplar of moral greatness, Lord Lansdowne wrote many years before the French Revolution: "I have seen for the first time in my life what I did not believe could exist, that is, a man *who is exempt from fear and from hope*, and who nevertheless is full of life and warmth. Nothing can disturb his peace; nothing is necessary to him, and he takes a lively interest in all that is good."

In a paper on a volume of miscellaneous prose essays by M. Laprade, M. Sainte-Beuve has this sentence: "What strikes me above all and everywhere is, that the author, whether he reasons or whether he addresses himself to literary history, only understands his own mode of being and his own individuality. Hereby he reveals to us that he is not a critic." The first paragraph of a keen critique on M. de Pontmartin ends thus: "To say of even those writers who are opposed to us nothing which their judicious friends do not already think and are obliged to admit, this is my highest ambition." Discussing the proper method of dealing with the past, he writes: "For myself I respect tradition and I like novelty: I am never happier than when I can succeed in reconciling them together." Of Hoffman he says, in a paper on literary criticism: "He has many of the qualities of a true critic, conscientiousness, independence, ideas, an opinion of his own." These sentences, with others of like import, are keys to the character of the volumes from which they are taken. The office of the critic M. Sainte-Beuve administers, not for temporary or personal ends, but with a disinterested sense of its elevation and its responsibilities. Through healthy sympathies and knowledge ample and ripe, through firm sense with artistic flexibility, through largeness of view and subtlety of insight, he enters upon it more than ordinarily empowered for its due discharge. He is at once what the French call *fin* and what the English call "sound." In literary work, in biographical work, in work æsthetical and critical, he delights, and he has a wide capacity of appropriation. The spirit of a book, a man, an age, he seizes quickly. With a nice perception of shades he catches the individual color of a mind or a production; and by the same faculty he grasps the determining principles in a character. Delicately, strongly, variously endowed, there is a steady equilibrium among his fine powers. Considering the bulk and vast variety and general excellence of his critical work, is it too much to say of him, that he is not only, as he has been called, the foremost of living critics, but that he deserves to hold the first place among all critics? No other has done so much so well. Goethe and Coleridge are something more; they are critics incidentally; but M. Sainte-Beuve, with poetical and philosophical qualities that lift him to a high vantage-ground, has made criticism his life-work, and through conscientious and symmetrical use of these qualities has done his work well. Besides much else in his many and many-sided volumes, there is to be read in them a full, spirited history of French literature.

Our attempt to make M. Sainte-Beuve better

known on this side the Atlantic we cannot more fitly conclude than with a sketch of him — a literary sketch — by himself. This we find in the fifth volume of the "Nouveaux Lundis," in a paper on Molière, published in July, 1863. A man who, in the autumnal ripeness of his powers, thus frankly tells us his likes and dislikes, tells us what he is. While by reflected action the passage becomes a self-portraiture, it is a sample of finest criticism.

"To make Molière loved by more people is in my judgment to do a public service.

"Indeed, to love Molière — I mean to love him sincerely and with all one's heart — it is, do you know? to have within one's self a guarantee against many defects, much wrong-headedness. It is, in the first place, to dislike what is incompatible with Molière, all that was counter to him in his day, and that would have been insupportable to him in ours.

"To love Molière is to be forever cured — I do not say of base and infamous hypocrisy, but of fanaticism, of intolerance, and of that kind of hardness which makes one anathematize and curse; it is to carry a corrective to admiration even of Bossuet, and for all who, after his example, exult, were it only in words, over their enemy dead or dying; who usurp I know not what holy speech, and involuntarily believe themselves to be, with the thunderbolt in their hand, in the region and place of the Most High. Men eloquent and sublime, you are far too much so for me!

"To love Molière, is to be sheltered against, and a thousand leagues away from, that other fanaticism, the political, which is cold, dry, cruel, which never laughs, which smells of the sectary, which, under pretext of Puritanism, finds means to mix and knead all that is bitter, and to combine in one sour doctrine the hates, the spites, and the Jacobinism of all times. It is to be not less removed, on the other hand, from those tame, dull souls who, in the very presence of evil, cannot be roused to either indignation or hatred.

"To love Molière, is to be secured against giving in to that pious and boundless admiration for a humanity which worships itself, and which forgets of what stuff it is made, and that, do what it will, it is always poor human nature. It is, not to despise it too much, however, this common humanity, at which one laughs, of which one is, and into which we throw ourselves through a healthful hilarity whenever we are with Molière.

"To love and cherish Molière, is to detest all mannerism in language and expression; it is, not to take pleasure in, or to be arrested by, petty graces, elaborate subtlety, superfine finish, excessive refinement of any kind, a tricky or artificial style.

"To love Molière, it is to be disposed to like neither false wit nor pedantic science; it is to know how to recognize at first sight our *Trissotins*[1] and our *Vadius* even under their rejuvenated jaunty airs; it is, not to let one's self be captivated at present any more than formerly by the everlasting *Philaminte*, that affected pretender of all times, whose form only changes and whose plumage is incessantly renewed; it is, to like soundness and directness of mind in others as well as in ourselves. I only give the first movement and the pitch; on this key one may continue, with variations.

"To love and openly to prefer Corneille, as certain minds do, is no doubt a fine thing, and, in one sense, a very legitimate thing; it is, to dwell in, and to mark one's rank in, the world of great souls: but is it not to run the risk of

[1] Trissotin, Vadius, and Philaminte, are personages in Molière's comedy of *Les Femmes Savantes* (The Blue-Stockings).

loving together with the grand and sublime, false glory a little, to go so far as not to detest inflation and magniloquence, an air of heroism on all occasions? He who passionately loves Corneille cannot be an enemy to a little boasting.

"On the other hand, to love and prefer Racine, ah! that is, no doubt, to love above all things, elegance, grace, what is natural and true (at least relatively), sensibility, touching and charming passion; but at the same time is it not also, to allow your taste and your mind to be too much taken with certain conventional and over-smooth beauties, a certain tameness and petted languidness, with certain excessive and exclusive refinements? In a word, to love Racine so much, it is to run the risk of having too much of what in France is called taste, and which brings so much distaste.

"To love Boileau — but no, one does not love Boileau, one esteems him, one respects him; we admire his uprightness, his understanding, at times his animation, and if we are tempted to love him, it is solely for that sovereign equity which made him do such unshaken justice to the great poets his contemporaries, and especially to him whom he proclaims the first of all, Molière.

"To love La Fontaine, is almost the same thing as to love Molière ; it is, to love nature, the whole of nature, humanity ingenuously depicted, a representation of the grand comedy "of a hundred different acts," unrolling itself, cutting itself up before our eyes into a thousand little scenes with the graces and freedoms that are so becoming, with weaknesses also. and liberties which are never found in the simple, manly genius of the master of masters. But why separate them ? La Fontaine and Molière — we must not part them, we love them united."

The number of "Putnam's Magazine," containing this paper, was sent to M. Sainte-Beuve accompanied by a note. In due time I received an answer to the note, saying that the Magazine had not reached him. Hereupon I sent the article by itself. On receiving it he wrote the following acknowledgment.

In my note I referred to a rumor of his illness. His disease was, by *post mortem* examination, discovered to be as the newspapers had reported, the stone. But a consultation of physicians declared that it was what he states it to be in his letter. Had they not made so gross a mistake, his life might have been prolonged.

"PARIS, 6 *Decbre,* 1868,
No. 11 Rue Mont Parnasse.

"CHER MONSIEUR : —

"Oh ! Cette fois je reçois bien décidément le très aimable et si bien etudié portrait du *critique.* Comment exprimer comme je le sens ma gratitude pour tant de soin, d'attention pénétrante, de désir d'être agréable tout en restant juste? Il y avait certes moyen d'insister bien plus sur les variations, les disparates et les défaillances momentanées de la pensée et du jugement à travers cette suite de volumes. C'est toujours un sujet d'étonnement pour moi, et cette fois autant que jamais, de voir comment un lecteur ami et un juge de gout parvient à tirer une figure une et consistante de ce qui ne me parait à moi même dans mon souvenir que le cours d'un long fleuve qui va s'épandant un peu au hazard des pentes et desertant continuellement ses rives. De tels portraits comme celui que vous voulez bien m'offrir me rendent un point d'appui et me feraient véritablement croire à moi-même. Et quand je songe a l'immense quantité d'esprits auxquels vous me présentez sous un aspect si favorable et si magistral dans ce nouveau monde de tant de jeunesse et d'avenir, je me prends d'une sorte de fierté et de courageuse confiance comme en présence déjà de la posterité.

"Le mal auquel vous voulez bien vous intéresser est tout simplement une hypertrophie de la prostate. Les souffrances ne sont pas vives, mais l'incommodité est grande, ne pouvant supporter à aucun degré le mouvement de la voiture, ce qui restreint ma vie sociale à un bien court rayon.

"Veuillez agreéer, cher Monsieur, l'assurance de ma cordiale gratitude, et de mes sentiments les plus distingués.

SAINTE-BEUVE."

VI.

THOMAS CARLYLE.

A BRAIN ever aglow with self-kindled fire — a cerebral battery bristling with magnetic life — such is Thomas Carlyle. Exceptional fervor of temperament, rare intellectual vivacity, manful earnestness — these are the primary qualifications of the man. He has an uncommon soul-power. Hence his attractiveness, hence his influence. Every page, every paragraph, every sentence, throbs with his own being. Themselves all authors put, of course, more or less, into what they write: few, very few, can make their sentences quiver with themselves. This Mr. Carlyle does by the intenseness of a warm individuality, by the nimble vigor of his mental life, and, be it added, by the rapture of his spirituality. The self, in his case, is a large, deep self, and it sends an audible pulse through his pen into his page.

To all sane men is allotted a complete endowment of mental faculties, of capacities of intellect and feeling; the degree to which these are energized, are injected with nervous flame, makes the difference between a genius and a blockhead. There being high vital pressure at a full, rich, interior source, and thence, strong mental currents, through what channels the currents shall flow depends on individual aptitudes, these aptitudes shaping, in the one case, a Dante, in another, a Newton, in another, a Mirabeau. And Nature, with all her generosity, being jealous of her rights, allows no interchange of gifts. Even the many-sided Goethe could not, by whatever force of will and practice, have written a bar in a symphony of Beethoven. In his dominant aptitudes, Mr. Carlyle is not more one-sided than many other intellectual potentates; but, like some others, his activity and ambition have at times led him into paths where great deficiencies disclose themselves by the side of great superiorities. His mind is biographical, not historical; stronger in details than in generalization; more intuitive than scientific; critical, not constructive; literary, not philosophical. Mr. Carlyle is great at a picture, very great; he can fail in a survey or an induction. Wealth of thought, strokes of tenderness, clean insight into life, satire, irony, humor, make his least successful volumes to teem with passages noteworthy, beautiful, wise, as do his "Cromwell" and his "Frederick." Such giants carrying nations on their broad fronts, Mr. Carlyle, in writing their lives with duteous particularity, has embraced the full story of the epoch in which each was the leader. To him they are more than leaders. Herein he and Mr. Buckle stand at opposite poles; Mr. Buckle underrating the protagonists of history, them and their share of agency; Mr. Carlyle overrating them, — a prejudicial one-sidedness in both cases. Leader and led are the complements the one of the other.

History is a growth, and a slow growth. Evils in one age painfully sow the seed that is to come up good in another. The historian, and still more the critical commentator on his own times, needs to be patient, calm, judicial, hopeful. Mr. Carlyle is impatient, fervid, willful, nay, despotic, and he is not hopeful, not hopeful enough. One healthily hopeful, and genuinely faithful, would not be ever betaking him to the past as a refuge from the present; would not tauntingly throw into the face of contemporaries an Abbot Sampson of the twelfth century as a model. A judicial expounder would not cite one single example as a characteristic of that age in contrast with this. A patient, impartial elucidator, would not deride "ballot-boxes, reform bills, winnowing machines:" he would make the best of these and other tools within reach; or, if his part be to write and not to act, would animate, not dishearten, those who are earnestly doing, and who, by boldly striking at abuses, by steadily striving for more justice, by aiming to lift up the down-trodden, prepare, through such means as are at hand, a better ground for the next generation. If to such workers, instead of God-speed, a writer of force and influence gives jeers and gibes, and ever-repeated shrieks about "semblance and quackery, and cant and speciosity, and dilettantism," and deems himself profound and original, as well as hopeful, when he exclaims: "Dim all souls of men to the divine, the high and awful meaning of human worth and truth, we shall never by all the machinery in Birmingham discover the true and worthy:" in that case, does he not expose him to the taunt of being himself very like a mouthing quack, and his words, which should be cordial, brotherly, do they not partake of the hollow quality of what Mr. Carlyle holds in such abhorrence, namely, of cant? The sick lion crouches growling in his lair; he cannot eat, and he will not let others eat.

Many grateful and admiring readers Mr. Carlyle wearies with his ever-recurrent fallacy that might is right. In Heaven's name, what are all the shams whose presence he so persistently bemoans, — worldly bishops, phantasm-aristocracies, presumptuous upstarts, shallow sway-wielding dukes, — what are all these, and much else, but so many exemplications of might that is not right? When might shall cease to bully, to trample on right, we shall be nearing Utopia. Utopia may be at infinite distance, not attainable by finite men; but as surely as our hearts beat, we are gradually getting further from its opposite, the coarse rule of force and brutality, such rule as in the twelfth century was rife all around "Abbot Sampson."

Like unto this moral fallacy is an æsthetic fallacy which, through bright pages of criticism, strikes up at times to vitiate a judgment. "I confess," says Mr. Carlyle, "I have no notion of a truly great man that could not be all sorts of men." Could Newton have written the "Fairy Queen?" Could Spenser have discovered the law of gravitation? Could Columbus have given birth to "Don Quixote?" One of Mr. Carlyle's military heroes tried hard to be a poet. Over Frederick's verses, how his friend Voltaire must have grinned. "I cannot understand how a Mirabeau, with that great glowing heart, with the fire that was in it, with the bursting tears that were in it, could not have written verses, tragedies, poems, and touched all hearts in that way, had his course of life and education led him thitherward." Thus Mr. Carlyle writes in "Heroes and Hero-Worship." If Mirabeau, why not Savonarola, or Marcus Aurelius. In that case a "Twelfth Night," or an "Othello," might have come from Luther. Nature does not work so loosely. Rich is she, unspeakably rich, and as artful as she is profuse in the use of her riches. She delights in variety, thence her ineffable radiance, and much of her immeasurable efficiency. Diverseness in unity is a source of her power as well as of her beauty. Her wealth of material being infinite, her specifications are endless, countless, superfinely minute. Even no two of the commonest men does she make alike; her men of genius she diversifies at once grandly and delicately, broadly and subtly. "Petrarch and Boccaccio did diplomatic messages," says Mr. Carlyle. We hope they did, or could have done, in the prosaic field, much better than that. We Americans know with what moderate equipment diplomatic messages may be done.

On poetry and poets Mr. Carlyle has written many of his best pages, pages penetrating, discriminative, because so sympathetic, and executed with the scholar's care and the critic's culture. His early papers on Goethe and Burns, published more than forty years ago, made something like an epoch in English criticism. Seizing the value and significance of genuine poetry, he exclaims in "Past and Present,"—"Genius, Poet! do we know what these words mean? An inspired soul once more vouchsafed us, direct from Nature's own great fire-heart, to see the truth, and speak it and do it." On the same page he thus taunts his countrymen: "We English find a poet, as brave a man as has been made for a hundred years or so anywhere under the sun; and do we kindle bonfires, thank the gods? Not at all. We, taking due counsel of it, set the man to gauge ale-barrels in the Burgh of Dumfries, and pique ourselves on our 'patronage of genius.'" "George the Third is Defender of something we call 'the Faith' in those years. George the Third is head charioteer of the destinies of England, to guide them through the gulf of French Revolutions, American Independences; and Robert Burns is gauger of ale in Dumfries." Poor George the Third! One needs not be a craniologist to know that the eyes which looked out from beneath that retreating pyramidal forehead could see but part even of the commonest men and things before them. How could they see a Robert Burns? To be sure, had Dundas, or whoever got Burns the place of gauger, given him one of the many sinecures of two or three hundred pounds a year that were wasted on idle scions of titled families, an aureole of glory would now shine through the darkness that environs the memory of George III. So much for George Guelf. Now for Thomas Carlyle.

If, for not recognizing Burns, *poor* George is to be blamed, what terms of stricture will be too harsh for *rich* Thomas, that by him were not recognized poets greater than Burns, at a time when for England's good, full, sympathetic recognition of them was just what was literarily most wanted? Here was a man, for the fine function of poetic criticism how rarely gifted is visible in those thorough papers on Burns and Goethe, written so early as 1828, wherein, besides a masterly setting forth of their great subjects, are notable passages on other poets. On Byron is passed the following sentence, which will, we think, be ever confirmed by sound criticism. "Generally speaking, we should say that Byron's poetry is not true. He refreshes us, not with the divine fountain, but too often with vulgar strong waters, stimulating indeed to the taste, but soon ending in dislike, or even nausea. Are his Harolds and Giaours, we would ask, real men ; we mean, poetically consistent and conceivable men ? Do not these characters, does not the character of their author, which more or less shines through them all, rather appear a thing put on for the occasion ; no natural or possible mode of being, but something intended to look much grander than nature ? Surely, all these stormful agonies, this volcanic heroism, superhuman contempt, and moody desperation, with so much scowling and teeth-gnashing, and other sulphurous humor, is more like the brawling of a player in some paltry tragedy, which is to last three hours, than the bearing of a man in the business of life, which is to last threescore and ten years.

To our minds, there is a taint of this sort, something which we should call theatrical, false, affected, in every one of these otherwise so powerful pieces."

In the same paper, that on Burns, Mr. Carlyle thus opened the ears of that generation, — partially opened, for the general æsthetic ear is not fully opened yet, — to a hollowness which was musical to the many: "Our Grays and Glovers seemed to write almost as if *in vacuo;* the thing written bears no mark of place; it is not written so much for Englishmen as for men; or rather, which is the inevitable result of this, for certain generalizations which philosophy termed men." And in the paper on Goethe, he calls Gray's poetry, "a laborious mosaic, through the hard, stiff lineaments of which, little life or true grace could be expected to look." Thus choicely endowed was Mr. Carlyle to be, what is the critic's noblest office, an interpreter between new poets and the public. Such an interpreter England grievously needed, to help and teach her educated and scholarly classes to prize the treasures just lavished upon them by Wordsworth, and Coleridge, and Shelley, and Keats. The interpreter was there, but he spoke not. Better than any man in England Mr. Carlyle could, if he would, have taught the generation that was growing up with him, whose ear he had already gained, what truth and fresh beauty and deep humanity there was in the strains of this composite chorus of superlative singers. Of such teaching, that generation stood in especial need, to disabuse its ear of the hollowness which had been mistaken for harmony; to refresh, with clear streams from "the divine fountain," hearts that were fevered by the stimulus of Byronic "strong waters;" to wave before half-awakened eyes the torch which lights the way to that higher plane where breathe great poets, whose incomparable function it is, to impart to their fellow-men some of the enlargement and the purification of consciousness in which themselves exult through the influx of fresh ideas and the upspringing of prolific sentiment. The gifted interpreter was dumb. Nay, he made diversions into Scotland and Germany, to bring Burns and Scott more distinctly before Englishmen, and to make Schiller and Goethe and Richter better known to them. And it pleased him to write about "Corn-law rhymes." That he did these tasks so well, proves how well he could have done, by the side of them, the then more urgent task. In 1828, Mr. Carlyle wrote for one of the quarterly reviews an exposition of "Goethe's Helena," which is a kind of episode in the second part of "Faust," and was first published as a fragment. This takes up more than sixty pages in the first volume of the "Miscellanies," about the half being translations from "Helena," which by no means stands in the front rank of Goethe's poetic creations, which is indeed rather a high artistic composition than a creation. At that time there lay, almost uncalled for, on the publisher's shelf, where it had lain for five years, ever since its issue, a poem of fifty-five Spenserian stanzas, flushed with a subtler beauty, more divinely dyed in pathos, than any in English literature of its rare kind, or of any kind out of Shakespeare, — a poem in which all the inward harvests of a tender, deep, capacious, loving, and religious life, all the heaped hoards of feeling and imagination in a life most visionary and most real, are gathered into one sheaf of poetic affluence, to dazzle and subdue with excess of light, — or gathered rather into a bundle of sheaves, stanza rising on stanza, each like a flame fresh shooting from a hidden bed of Nature's most precious perfumes, each shedding a new and a richer fragrance; I mean the "Adonais" of Shelley. For this glittering masterpiece, — a congenial commentary on which would have illuminated the literary atmosphere of England, — Mr. Carlyle had no word; no word for Shelley, no word for Coleridge, no word for Wordsworth. For Keats he had a word in the paper on Burns, and here it is: "Poetry, except in such cases as that of Keats, where the whole consists in a weak-eyed, maudlin sensibility, and a certain vague, random timefulness of nature, is no separate faculty." A parenthesis, short and contemptuous, is all he gives to one of whom it has been truly said, that of no poet who has lived, not of Shakespeare, is the poetry written before the twenty-fifth year so good as his; and of whom it may as truly be said, that his best poems need no apology in the youthfulness of their author; but that for originality, power, variety, feeling, thoughtfulness, melody, they take rank in the first class of the poetry of the world. Is not Thomas Carlyle justly chargeable with having committed a high literary misdemeanor? Nay, considering his gift of poetic insight, and with it his persistent ignoring of the great English poets of his age, considering the warm solicitation on the one side, and the duty on the other, his offense may be termed a literary crime. He knew better.

Mr. Carlyle somewhere contrasts his age with that of Elizabeth, after this fashion ; "For Raleighs and Shakespeares we have Beau Brummell and Sheridan Knowles." Only on the surmise that Mr. Carlyle owed poor Knowles some desperate grudge, can such an outburst be accounted for. Otherwise it is sheer fatuity, or an impotent explosion of literary spite. For the breadth and brilliancy of the poetic day shed upon it, no period in the history of any nation, not that of Pericles or of Elizabeth, is more resplendent than that which had not yet faded for England when Mr. Carlyle began his career ; nor in the field of public action can the most prolific era of Greece or of England hold up, for the admiration of the world and the pride of fellow-countrymen, two agents more deservedly crowned with honor and gratitude than Nelson and Wellington. Here are two leaders, who, besides exhibiting rare personal prowess and quick-eyed military genius on fields of vast breadth, and in performances of unwonted magnitude and momentousness, were, moreover, by their great, brave deeds, most palpably saving England, saving Europe, from the grasp of an inexorable despot. Surely these were heroes of a stature to have strained to its utmost the reverence and the love of a genuine hero-worshipper. On the ten thousand luminous pages of Mr. Carlyle they find no place. Not only are their doings not celebrated, that they lived is scarce acknowledged.

Even when its objects are the loftiest and the most honored, jealousy is not a noble form of

"The last infirmity of noble mind."

Does Mr. Carlyle feel that Nelson and Wellington, Coleridge, Shelley, Keats, and Wordsworth, stand already so broad and high that they chill him with their shadow, and that therefore he will not, by eulogy, or even notice, add to their altitude? Is he repeating the littleness of Byron, who was jealous not only of his contemporaries, Napoleon, and Wellington, and Wordsworth, but was jealous of Shakespeare? That a pen which, with zestful animation, embraces all contemporaneous things, should be studiously silent about almost every one of the dozen men of genius who illustrate his era, is a fact so monstrous, that one is driven to monstrous devices to divulge its motive. In such a case it is impossible to premise to what clouds of self-delusion an imaginative man will not rise.

Writing of Thomas Carlyle, the last words must not be censorious comments on a weakness; we all owe too much to his strength; he is too large a benefactor. Despite over-fondness for Frederick and the like, and what may be termed a pathological drift towards political despotism, how many quickening chapters has he not added to the "gospel of freedom"? Flushed are his volumes with generous pulses, with delicate sympathies. From many a page what cordialities step forth to console and to fortify us; what divine depths we come upon; what sudden vistas of sunshine through tempest-shaken shadows; what bursts of splendor through nebulous mutterings. Much has he helped the enfranchisement of the spirit. Well do I remember the thirst wherewith, more than thirty years ago, I seized the monthly "Frazer," to drink of the spiritual waters of "Sartor Resartus." Here was a new spring; with what stimulating, exhilarating, purifying draughts, did it bubble and sparkle! That picture, in the beginning, of the "doing and driving (*Thun und*

Treiben)" of a city as beheld by Professor Teufelsdroeckh from his attic — would one have been surprised to read that on a page of Shakespeare?

A marvelous faculty of speech has Mr. Carlyle; a gift of saying what he has to say with a ring in the words that makes the thought tingle through your ears. His diction surrounds itself with a magnetic *aura*, which seems to float it, to part it from the paper, it stands out in such transparent chiar-oscuro. Common phrases he refreshes by making them the vehicle for new meanings, and in the ordering of words he has command of a magical logic. The marrowy vigor in his mind it is that lends such expressiveness, such nimbleness, such accent to his sentences, to his style.

Mr. Carlyle's power comes mainly from his sensibilities. Through them he is poetical; through them there is so much light in his pages. More often from his than from any others, except those of the major poets, breaks the sudden, joyful beam that flames around a thought when it knows itself embraced by a feeling. Of humor and of wit, what an added fund does our language now possess through his pen. The body of criticism, inclosed in the five volumes of Miscellanies, were enough to give their author a lasting name. When one of these papers appeared in the Edinburgh, or other review, it shone, amid the contributions of the Jeffreys and Broughams, like a guinea in a handful of shillings.

The masterpiece of Mr. Carlyle, and the masterpiece of English prose literature, is his "French Revolution," a rhythmic Epic without verse. To write those three volumes a man needs have in him a big, glowing heart, thus to flood with passionate life all the men and scenes of a momentous volcanic epoch ; a lively, strong, intellectual vision he must have, to grasp in their full reality the multitudinous and diverse facts and incidents so swiftly begotten under the pulsation of millions of contentious brains ; he needs a literary faculty finely artistic, creatively imaginative, to enrank the figures of such vast tumultuous scenes, to depict the actors in each, to present vividly in clear relief the rapid succession of eventful convulsions. Outside of the choice achievements of verse, is there a literary task of breadth and difficulty that has been done so well ? A theme of unusual grandeur and significance is here greatly treated.

The foremost literary gift, — nay, the test whereby to try whether there be any genuine literary gift, — is the power in a writer to impart so much of himself, that his subject shall stand invested, or rather, imbued, with a life which renews it; it becomes warmed with a fire from the writer's soul. Of this, the most perfect exhibition is in poetry, wherein, by the intensity and fullness of inflammation, of passion, is born a something new, which, through the strong creativeness of the poet, has henceforth a rounded being of its own. With this power Mr. Carlyle is highly endowed. Not only, as already said, does his page quiver with himself; through the warmth and healthiness of his sympathies, and his intellectual mastery, he makes each scene and person in his gorgeous representation of the French Revolution to shine with its own life, the more brilliantly and truly that this life has been lighted up by his. Where in history is there a picture greater than that of the execution of Louis XVI.? With a few strokes how many a vivid portrait does he paint, and each one vivid chiefly from its faithfulness to personality and to history. And then his full-length, more elaborated likenesses, of the king, of the queen, of the Duke of Orleans, of Lafayette, of Camille Desmoulins, of Danton, of Robespierre: it seems now that only on his throbbing page do these personages live and move and have their true being. The giant Mirabeau, 'twas thought at first he had drawn too gigantic. But intimate documents, historical and biographical, that have come to light since, confirm the insight of Mr. Carlyle, and swell his hero out to the large proportions he has given him.

For a conclusion we will let Mr. Carlyle depict himself. Making allowance for some humorous play in describing a fellow-man so eccentric as his friend, Professor Teufelsdroeckh, this we think he does consciously and designedly in the fourth chapter of "Sartor Resartus," wherein, under the head of "Characteristics," he comments on the professor's Work on Clothes, and its effect on himself. From this chapter we extract some of the most pertinent sentences. It opens thus: —

"It were a piece of vain flattery to pretend that this Work on Clothes entirely contents us; that it is not, like all works of genius, like the very sun, which, though the highest published creation, or work of genius, has nevertheless black spots and troubled nebulosities amid its effulgence, — a mixture of insight, inspiration, with dullness' double-vision, and even utter blindness.

"Without committing ourselves to those enthusiastic praises and prophesyings of the "Weissnichtwo'sche Anzeiger," we admitted that the book had in a high degree excited us to self-activity, which is the best effect of any book; that it had even operated changes in our way of thought; nay, that it promised to prove, as it were, the opening of a new mine-shaft, wherein the whole world of *Speculation* might henceforth dig to unknown depths. More especially it may now be declared that Professor Teufelsdroeckh's acquirements, patience of research, philosophic, and even poetic vigor, are here made indisputably manifest; and unhappily no less his prolixity and tortuosity and manifold inaptitude. . . .

"Many a deep glance, and often with unspeakable precision, has he cast into mysterious Nature, and the still more mysterious Life of man. Wonderful it is with what cutting words, now and then, he severs asunder the confusion; sheers down, were it furlongs deep, into the true center of the matter; and there not only hits the nail on the head, but with crushing force smites it home and buries it. . . .

"Occasionally, as above hinted, we find consummate vigor, a true inspiration; his burning thoughts step forth in fit burning words, like so many full-formed Minervas, issuing amid flame and splendor from Jove's head; a rich idiomatic diction, picturesque allusions, fiery poetic emphasis, or quaint tricksy twins; all the graces and terrors of a wild imagination, wedded to the clearest intellect, alternate in beautiful vicissitude. Were it not that sheer sleeping and soporific passages, circumlocutions, repetitions, touches even of pure doting jargon so often intervene. . . . . A wild tone pervades the whole utterance of the man, like its key-note and regulator; now screwing itself aloft as into the Song of Spirits, or else the shrill mockery of fiends; now sinking in cadences, not without melodious heartiness, though sometimes abrupt enough, into the common pitch, when we hear it only as a monotonous hum; of which hum the true character is extremely difficult to fix. . . .

"Under a like difficulty, in spite even of our personal intercourse, do we still lie with regard to the professor's moral feeling. Gleams of an ethereal love burst forth from him, soft wailings of infinite pity; he could clasp the whole universe into his bosom, and keep it warm; it seems as if under that rude exterior there dwelt a very seraph. Then, again, he is so sly, and still so imperturbably saturnine; shows such indifference, malign coolness, towards all that men strive after; and ever with some half-visible wrinkle of a bitter, sardonic humor, if indeed it be not mere stolid callousness, — that you look on him almost with a shudder, as on some incarnate Mephistopheles, to whom this great terrestrial and celestial Round, after all, were but some huge foolish whirligig, where kings and beggars, and angels and demons, and stars and street-sweepings, were chaotically whirled, in which only children could take interest."

VII.

ERRATA.[1]

WORDS are the counters of thought; speech is the vocalization of the soul; style is the luminous incarnation of reason and emotion. Thence it behooves scholars, the wardens of language, to keep over words a watch as keen and sleepless as a dutiful guardian keeps over his pupils. A prime office of this guardianship is to take care lest language fall into loose ways; for words being the final elements into which all speech resolves itself, if they grow weak by negligence or abuse, speech loses its firmness, veracity, and expressiveness. Style may be likened to a close Tyrian garment woven by poets and thinkers out of words and phrases for the clothing and adornment of the mind; and the strength and fineness of the tissue, together with its beauties of color, depend on the purity and precision, the transparency and directness of its threads, which are words.

[1] From Lippincott's Magazine, 1870.

A humble freeman of the guild of scholars would here use his privilege to call attention to some abuses in words and pnrases, — abuses which are not only prevalent in the spoken and written speech of the many, but which disfigure, occasionally, the pages, even of good writers. These are not errors that betoken or lead to general final corruption, and the great Anglo-Saxo-Norman race is many centuries distant from the period when it may be expected to show signs of that decadence which, visible at first in the waning moral and intellectual energies of a people, soon spots its speech.

Nevertheless, as inaccuracies, laxities, vulgarisms — transgressions more or less superficial — such errors take from the correctness, from the efficacy, from the force as well as the grace, of written or spoken speech.

The high level of strength, suppleness and beauty occupied by our English tongue has been reached, and can only be maintained, by strenuous, varied, and continuous mental action. Offenses against the laws and proprieties of language — like so many other of our lapses — are in most cases effects of the tendency in human nature to relax its tone. None save the most resolute and rigorous but have their moods of unwatchfulness, of indolence. Moreover, men are prone to resist mental refinement and intellectual subdivisions. Discrimination requires close attention and sustained effort; and without habitual discrimination there can be no linguistic precision or excellence. In this, as in other provinces, people like to take things easily. Now, every capable man of business knows that to take things easily is an easy way to ruin. Language is in a certain sense every one's business; but it is especially the business, as their appellation denotes, of men of letters; and a primary duty of their high vocation is to be jealous of any careless or impertinent meddling with, or mishandling of, those little glistening, marvelous tools wherewith such amazing structures and temples have been built and are ever a-building. Culture, demanding and creating diversity and subtlety of mental processes, is at once a cause and an effect of infinite multiplication in the relations the mind is capable of establishing between itself and the objects of its action, and between its own processes; and language, being a chief instrument of culture, has to follow and subserve these multiplied and diversified demands. Any fall, therefore, on its part from the obedient fineness of its modes and modulations back into barbaric singleness and crudeness, any slide into looseness or vagueness, any unweaving of the complex tissue, psychical and metaphysical, into which it has been wrought by the exquisite wants of the mind, will have a relaxing, debilitating influence on thought itself. To use the clear, wise words of Mr. Whewell; "Language is often called an instrument of thought, but it is also the nutriment of thought; or, rather, it is the atmosphere on which thought lives — a medium essential to the activity of our speculative powers, although invisible and imperceptible in its operation; and an element modifying, by its changes and qualities, the growth and complexion of the faculties which it feeds."

Our enumeration of *errata* being made alphabetically, the first to be cited is one of the chief of sinners — the particle.

As. The misuse of *as* for *so* is, in certain cases, almost universal. If authority could justify error and convert the faulty into the faultless, it were idle to expose a misuse in justification of which can be cited most of the best names in recent English literature.

"*As* far as doth concern my single self,"

is a line in Wordsworth ("Prelude," p. 70) which, by a change of the first *as* into *so*, would gain not only in sound (which is not our affair at present), but likewise in grammar. The seventh line of the twenty-first stanza in that most tender of elegies and most beautiful of poems, Shelley's "Adonais," begins, "*As* long as skies are blue," where also there would be a double gain by writing "*So* long as skies are blue." On page 242 of the first volume of De Quincey's "Literary Remains" occurs this sentence; "Even by *as* philosophic a politican *as* Edmund Burke," in which the critical blunder of calling Burke a philosophic politician furnishes no excuse for the grammatical blunder. The rule (derived, like all good rules, from principle) which determines the use of this small particle is, I conceive, that the double *as* should only be employed when there is direct comparison. In the first part of the following sentence there is no direct comparative relation — in the second, the negative destroys it; "*So* far as geographical measurement goes, Philadelphia is not *so* far from New York as from Baltimore." Five writers out of six would commit the error of using *as* in both members of the sentence. The most prevalent misuse of *as* is in connection with *soon;* and this general misuse, having moreover the countenance of good writers, is so inwoven into our speech that it will be hard to unravel it. But principle is higher than the authority derived from custom. Judges are bound to give sentence according to the statute; and if the highest writers, whose influence is deservedly judicial, violate the laws of language, their decisions ought to be, and will be, reversed, or language will be undermined, and, slipping into shallow, illogical habits, into anarchical conditions, will forfeit much of its manliness, of its subtlety, of its truthfulness. Language is a living organism, and to substitute authority, or even long usage, for its innate genius and wisdom, and the requirements and practices that result from these, were to strike at its life, and to expose it to become subject to upstart usurpation, to deadening despotism. Worcester quotes from the Psalms the phrase, "They go astray *as* soon as they be born." We ask, Were not the translators of the Bible as liable to err in grammar as De Quincey, or Wordsworth, or Shelley? A writer in the English "National Review" for January, 1862, in an admirable paper on the "Italian Clergy and the Pope," begins a sentence with the same phrase:

"*As* soon as the law was passed." And we ourselves, sure though we be that the use of *as* in this and every similar position is an error, need to brace both pen and tongue against running into it, so strong to overcome principle and conviction is the habit of the senses, accustomed daily to see and to hear the wrong.

AT THAT. We should not have noticed this squat vulgarism, had not the pen blazoned its own depravity by lifting it out of newspapers into bound volumes. The speech and page of every one, who would not be italicized for lingual looseness, should be forever closed against a phrase so shocking to taste, a phrase, we are sorry to say, of American mintage, coined in one of those frolicksome exuberant moods, when a young people, like a loosed horse full of youth and oats, kicks up and scatters mud with the unharnessed license of his heels.

ANOTHER. Before passing to the letter B on our alphabetical docket, we will call up a minor criminal in A, viz. *another*, often incorrectly used for *other;* as in "on one ground or another," "from one cause or another." Now, *another*, the prefix *an* making it singular, — embraces but one ground or cause, and therefore, contrary to the purpose of the writer, the words mean that there are but two grounds or causes. Write "on one ground or other," and the words are in harmony with the meaning of the writer, the word *other* implying several or many grounds.

BOQUET. The sensibility that gives the desire to preserve a present sparkling so long as is possible with all the qualities that made it materially acceptable, should rule us where the gift is something so precious as a word; and when we receive one from another people, gratitude, as well as sense of grace in the form of the gift itself, should make us watchful that it be not dimmed by the boorish breath of ignorance or cacophanized by unmusical voices. We therefore protest against a useful and tuneful noun-substantive, a native of France, the word *bouquet,* being maimed into *boquet,* a corruption as dissonant to the ear as were to the eye plucking a rose from a variegated nosegay, and leaving only its thorny stem. *Boquet* is heard at times in well-upholstered drawing-rooms, and may even be seen in print. Offensive in its mutilated shape, it smells sweet again when restored to its native orthography.

BY NO MANNER OF MEANS. The most vigorous writers are liable, in unguarded moments, to lapse into verbal weakness, and so you meet with this vulgar pleonasm in Ruskin.

By reason of. An ill-assorted, ugly phrase, used by accomplished reviewers and others, who ought to set a purer example.

Come off. Were a harp to give out the nasal whine of the bagpipe, or the throat of a nightingale to emit the caw of a raven, the æsthetic sense would not be more startled and offended than to hear from feminine lips, rosily wreathed by beauty and youth, issue the words, "The concert will *come off* on Wednesday." This vulgarism should never be heard beyond the "ring" and the cock-pit, and should be banished from resorts so respectable as an oyster-cellar.

Consider. Neither weight of authority nor universality of use can purify or justify a linguistic corruption, and make the intrinsically wrong in language right; and therefore such phrases as, "I consider him an honest man," "Do you consider the dispute settled?" will ever be bad English, however generally sanctioned. In his dedication of the "Diversions of Purley" to the University of Cambridge, Horne Tooke uses it wrongly when he says, "who always *considers* acts of voluntary justice toward himself as favors." The original signification and only proper use of *consider* are in phrases like these: "If you consider the matter carefully;" "Consider the lilies of the field."

CONDUCT. It seems to us that it were as allowable to say of a man, "He carries well," as "He conducts well." We say of a gun that it carries well, and we might say of a pipe that it conducts well. The gun and pipe are passive instruments, not living organisms, and thence the verbs are used properly in the neuter form. Perhaps, strictly speaking, even here *its charge* and *water* are understood.

CONTEMPLATE. "Do you contemplate going to Washington to-morrow?" "No: I contemplate moving into the country." This is more than exaggeration and inflation: it is desecration of a noble word, born of man's higher being; for contemplation is an exercise of the very highest faculties, a calm collecting of them for silent meditation — an act, or rather a mood, which implies even more than concentrated reflection, and involves themes dependent on large, pure sentiment. An able lawyer has to reflect much upon a broad, difficult case in order to master it; but when in the solitude of his study he is drawn, by the conflicts and wrongs he has witnessed during the day, to think on the purposes and destiny of human life, he more than reflects — he is lifted into a contemplative mood. Archbishop Trench, in his valuable volume on the "Study of Words," opens a paragraph with this sentence: "Let us now proceed to *contemplate* some of the attestations for God's truth, and some of the playings into the hands of the devil's falsehood, which may be found to lurk in words." Here we suggest that the proper word were *consider;* for there is activity, and a progressive activity, in the mental operation on which he enters, which disqualifies the verb *contemplate.*

Habitual showiness in language, as in dress and manners, denotes lack of discipline or lack of refinement. Our American magniloquence — the tendency to which is getting more and more subdued — comes partly from national youthfulness, partly from license, that bastard of liberty, and partly from the geographical and the present, and still more the prospective, political grandeur of the country, which Coleridge somewhere says is to be "England in glorious magnification."

I AM FREE TO CONFESS. An irredeemable vulgarism.

IN THIS CONNECTION. Another.

INDEBTEDNESS. "The amount of my *engagedness*" sounds as well and is as proper as "the amount of my *indebtedness*." We have already *hard-heartedness*, *wickedness*, *composedness*, and others. Nevertheless, this making of nouns out of adjectives with the participial form is an irruption over the boundaries of the parts of speech which should not be encouraged.

Archbishop Whately, in a passage of his short-coming comments on Bacon's "Essays," uses *preparedness*. Albeit that brevity is a cardinal virtue in writing, a circumlocution would, we think, be better than a gawky word like this, so unsteady on its long legs. In favor of *indebtedness* over others of like coinage, this is to be said — that it imports that which in one form or other comes home to the bosom of all humanity.

INTELLECTS. That man's intellectual power is not one and indivisible, but consists of many separate, independent faculties, is a momentous truth, revealed by the insight of Gall. One of the results of this great discovery may at times underlie the plural use of the important word *intellect* when applied to one individual. If so, it were still indefensible. It has, we suspect, a much less philosophic origin, and proceeds from the unsafe practice of overcharging the verbal gun in order to make more noise in the ear of the listener. The plural is correctly used when we speak of two or more different men.

LEFT. "I left at ten o'clock." This use of *leave* as a neuter verb, however attractive from its brevity, is not defensible. *To leave off* is the only proper neuter form. "We left off at six, and left (the hall) at a quarter past six." The place should be inserted after the second *left.* Even the first is essentially active, some form of action being understood after *off:* we left off *work* or *play.*

MIDST. "In our midst" is a common but incorrect phrase.

OUR AUTHOR. A vulgarism, which, by its seeming convenience, gets the countenance of critical writers. We say *seeming* convenience; for in this seeming lies the vulgarity, the writer expressing, unconsciously often, by the *our*, a feeling of patronage. With his *our* he pats the author on the back.

PERIODICAL is an adjective, and its use as a substantive is an unwarrantable gain of brevity at the expense of grammar.

PROPOSE. Hardly any word that we have

cited is so frequently misused, and by so many good writers, as *propose*, when the meaning is to design, to intend to propose. It should always be followed by a personal accusative — I propose to you, to him, to myself. In the preface to Hawthorne's "Marble Faun" occurs the following sentence; "The author *proposed* to himself merely to write a fanciful story, evolving a thoughtful moral, and did not *purpose* attempting a portraiture of Italian manners and character" — a sentence than which a fitter could not be written to illustrate the proper use of *propose* and *purpose*.

Predicated upon. This abomination is paraded by persons who lose no chance of uttering "dictionary words," hit or miss; and is sometimes heard from others from whom the educated world has a right to look for more correctness.

Reliable. A counterfeit, which no stamping by good writers or universality of circulation will ever be able to introduce into the family circle of honest English as a substitute for the robust Saxon word whose place it would usurp — *trustworthy*. *Reliable* is, however, good English when used to signify that one is liable again. When you have lost a receipt, and cannot otherwise prove that a bill rendered has been paid, you are *re-liable* for the amount.

RELIGION. Even by scholars this word is often used with looseness. In strictness it expresses exclusively our relation to the Infinite, the *bond* between man and God. You will sometimes read that he is the truly religious man who most faithfully performs his duties of neighbor, father, son, husband, citizen. However much a religious man may find himself strengthened by his faith and inspirited for the performance of all his duties, this strength is an indirect, and not a uniform or necessary, effect of religious convictions. Some men who are sincere in such convictions fail in these duties conspicuously; while, on the other hand, they are performed, at times, with more than common fidelity by men who do not carry within them any very lively religious belief or impressions. "And now abideth faith, hope, and charity, these three; but the greatest of these is charity." Nor can the greatest do the work of the others any more than faith that of hope or charity. Each one of "these three" is different from and independent of the other, however each one be aided by coöperation from the others. The deep, unique feeling which lifts up and binds the creature to the Creator is elementarily one in the human mind, and the word used to denote it should be kept solely for this high office, and not weakened or perverted by other uses. Worcester quotes from Dr. Watts the following sound definition : " In a proper sense, *virtue* signifies duty toward men, and *religion* duty to God."

SALOON. That eminent pioneer of American sculpture, brilliant talker, and accomplished gentleman, the lamented Horatio Greenough, was indignantly eloquent against the American abuse of this graceful importation from France, applied as it is in the United States to public billiard-rooms, oyster-cellars and grog-shops.

SUBJECT-MATTER. A tautological humpback.

TO VENTILATE, applied to a subject or person. The scholar who should use this vilest of vulgarisms deserves to have his right thumb taken off.

We have here noted a score of the errors prevalent in written and spoken speech — some of them perversions or corruptions, countenanced even by eminent writers ; some, misapplications that weaken and disfigure the style of him who adopts them ; and some, downright vulgarisms — that is, phrases that come from below, and are thrust into clean company with the odors of slang about them. These last are often a device for giving piquancy to style. Against such abuses we should be the more heedful, because, from the convenience of some of them, they get so incorporated into daily speech as not to be readily distinguishable from their healthy neighbors, clinging for generations to tongues and pens. Of this tenacity there is a notable exemplification in a passage of Boswell, written nearly a hundred years ago. Dr. Johnson found fault with Boswell for using the phrase to *make* money: "Don't you see the impropriety of it? To *make* money is to *coin* it: you should say *get* money." Johnson, adds Boswell, "was jealous of infractions upon the genuine English language, and prompt to repress colloquial barbarisms; such as *pledging* myself, for *undertaking; line* for *department* or *branch,* as the *civil line,* the *banking line.* He was particularly indignant against the almost universal use of the word *idea* in the sense of *notion* or *opinion,* when it is clear that *idea* can only signify something of which an image can be formed in the mind. We may have an *idea* or *image* of a mountain, a tree, a building, but we surely cannot have an idea or image of an *argument* or *proposition.* Yet we hear the sages of the law 'delivering their *ideas* upon the question under consideration;' and the first speakers of Parliament 'entirely coinciding in the *idea* which has been ably stated by an honorable member.'"

Whether or not the word *idea* may be properly used in a deeper or grander sense than that stated by Dr. Johnson, there is no doubt that he justly condemned its use in the cases cited by him, and in similar ones. All the four phrases *make money*, *pledge*, *line*, and *idea*, whereupon sentence of guilty was passed by the great lexicographer, are still at large, and, if it be not a bull to say so, more at large to-day than in the last century, since the area of their currency has been extended to America, Australia, and the Pacific Islands.

VIII.

A NATIONAL DRAMA.[1]

We are eminently a people of action; we are fond of shows, processions, and organized spectacles; we are so much more imitative than our British cousins, that, without limiting its appeals to the mimetic files of fashion, the ungentlemanly theory of a Simian descent for man might find support in the features of our general life. To complete the large compound of qualities that are required, in order that an emulous people give birth to a drama, one is yet wanting; but that one is not merely the most important of all, but is the one which lifts the others into dramatic importance. Are we poetical? Ask any number of continental Europeans, whether the English are a poetical people. A loud, unanimous, derisive *no* would be the answer. And yet, there is Shakespeare! and around him, back to Chaucer and forward to Tennyson, a band of such poets, that this

[1] From *Putnam's Monthly*, 1857.

prosaic nation has the richest poetic literature in Christendom. Especially in this matter are appearances delusive, and hasty inferences liable to be illogical. From the prosers that one hears in pulpits, legislatures, lecture-rooms, at morning calls and well-appointed dinner-tables in Anglo-America, let no man infer against our poetic endowment. Shakespeare, and Milton, and Burns, and Wordsworth, are of our stock; and what we have already done in poetry and the plastic arts, while yet, as a nation, hardly out of swaddling-clothes, is an earnest of a creative future. We are to have a national literature and a national drama. What is a national drama? Premising that as little in their depth as in their length will our remarks be commensurate with the dimensions of this great theme, we would say a few words.

A literature is the expression of what is warmest and deepest in the heart of a people. Good books are the crystallization of thoughts and feelings. To have a literature — that is, a body of enduring books — implies vigor and depth. Such books are the measure of the mental vitality in a people. Those peoples that have the best books will be found to be at the top of the scale of humanity; those that have none, at the bottom. Good books, once brought forth, exhale ever after both fragrance and nourishment. They educate while they delight many generations.

Good books are the best thoughts of the best men. They issue out of deep hearts and strong heads; and where there are deep hearts and strong heads such books are sure to come to life. The mind, like the body, will reproduce itself: the mind, too, is procreative, transmitting itself to a remote posterity.

The best books are the highest products of human effort. Themselves the evidence of creative power, they kindle and nourish power. Consider what a spring of life to European people have been the books of the Hebrews. What so precious treasure has England as Shakespeare?

To be good, books must be generic. They may be, in subject, in tone, and in color, national; but in substance they must be so universally human, that other cognate nations can imbibe and be nourished by them. Not that, in their fashioning, this fitness for foreign minds is to be a conscious aim; but to be thus attractive and assimilative, is a proof of their breadth and depth — of their high humanity.

The peoples who earliest reached the state of culture which is needed to bring forth books, each standing by itself, each necessarily sang and wrote merely of itself. Thus did the Hebrews and the Greeks. But already the Romans went out of themselves, and Virgil takes a Trojan for his hero. This appropriation of foreign material shows that the aim of high books is, to ascend to the sphere of ideas and feelings that are independent of time and place. Thence, when, by multiplication of Christian nations our mental world had become vastly enlarged, embracing in one bond of culture, not only all modern civilized peoples, but also the three great ancient ones, the poets — especially the dramatic, for reasons that will be presently stated — looked abroad and afar for the frame-work and corporeal stuff of their writings.

The most universal of all writers, ancient or modern, he who is most generic in his thought, Shakespeare, embodied his transcendent conceptions for the most part in foreign personages. Of Shakespeare's fourteen comedies, the scene of only one is laid in England; and that one, "The Merry Wives of Windsor" — the only one not written chiefly or largely in verse — is a

Shakespearean farce. Of the tragedies (except the series of the ten historical ones) only two, "Lear" and "Macbeth," stand on British ground. Is "Hamlet" on that score less English than "Lear," or "Othello" than "Macbeth"? Does Italy count Juliet among her trophies, or Desdemona?

Of Milton's two dramas — to confine myself here to the dramatic domain — the tragedy ("Samson Agonistes,") like his epics, is Biblical; the comedy ("Comus") has its home in a sphere

> "Above the smoke and stir of this dim spot
> Which men call earth."

Of the numerous athletic corps of dramatists, contemporary with Shakespeare and Milton, few have left works pithy enough and so poetically complete as to withstand the wear of time and keep fresh to each successive generation. But if you inspect the long list from which Charles Lamb took his "Specimens," you will find few British names.

Casting our eyes on the dramatic efforts of the recent English poetic celebrities, we perceive that Byron, Coleridge, and Shelley, all abandoned, in every instance, native ground. The only dramatic work of a great modern, the scene of which is laid within the British limits, is "The Borderers," of Wordsworth, which, though having the poetic advantage of remoteness in time — being thrown back to the reign of Henry III. — is, in strictness, neither a drama nor a poem, Wordsworth's deficiency in dramatic gifts being so signal as to cause, by the impotent struggle in an uncongenial element, a partial paralysis even of his high poetic genius.

Glance now across the Channel. French poetic tragedy is in its subjects almost exclusively ancient — Greek, Roman, and Biblical. In the works of the great comic genius of France, Molière, we have a salient exception to the practice of all other eminent dramatists. The scene of his plays is Paris; the time is the year in which each was written.

Let us look for the cause of this remarkable isolation.

Molière was the manager of a theatrical company in the reign of Louis XIV., and he wrote, as he himself declares, to please the king and amuse the Parisians. But deeper than this; Molière was by nature a great satirist. I call him a *great* satirist, because of the affluence of inward substance that fed his satiric appetite — namely, a clear, moral sensibility, distinguishing by instinct the true from the false, rare intellectual nimbleness, homely common sense, shrewd insight into men, a keen wit, with vivid perception of the comic and absurd. For a satirist so variously endowed, the stage was the best field, and for Molière especially, gifted as he was with histrionic genius. The vices and abuses, the follies and absurdities, the hypocrisies and superficialities of civilized life, these were the game for his faculties. The interior of Paris households he transferred to the stage with biting wit, doubling the attractiveness of his pictures by comic hyperbole. His portraits are caricatures, not because they exaggerate vices or foibles, but because they so bloat out a single personage with one vice or one folly as to make him a lop-sided deformity. Characters he did not seek to draw, but he made a personage the medium of incarnating a quality. Harpagon is not a miser ; he is Avarice speaking and doing. Alceste is not a person ; he is Misanthropy personified.

This fundamental exaggeration led to and facilitated the caricature of relations and juxtapositions. With laughable unscrupulousness Molière multiplies improbable blunders and conjunctions. All verisimilitude is sacrificed to scenic vivacity. Hence, the very highest of his comedies are farce-like ; even "Tartuffe" is so.

In Molière little dramatic growth goes on before the spectator's eye. His personages are not gradually built up by successive touches, broad or fine; they do not evolve themselves chiefly by collision with others; in the first act they come on the stage unfolded. The action and plot advance rapidly, but not through the unrolling of the persons represented. Hence, his most important personages are prosaic and finite. They interest you more as agents for the purpose in hand than as men and women. They are subordinate rather to the action than creative of action.

Molière is a most thorough realist, and herein is his strength. In him the comic is a vehicle for satire; and the satire gives pungency and body to the comic. He was primarily a satirist, secondarily a poet. Such being his powers and his aims, helpful to him, nay, needful, was a present Parisian actuality of story and agents. A poetic comedy ought to be, and will necessarily be, a chapter of very high life. Molière's comedies, dealing unctuously with vice and folly, are, philosophically speaking, low life. His are comedies not of character and sentiment, but of manners and morals, and therefore cannot be highly poetical; and thence he felt no want of a remote ground, clean of all local coloring and association, such as is essential to the dramatist whose inspiration is poetical, and who therefore must reconcile the ideal with the real, by which reconciliation only can be produced the purest truth. That, notwithstanding they belong not to the highest poetic sphere, his comedies continue to live and to be enjoyed, this testifies of the breadth and truthfulness of his humanity, the piercing insight of his rich mind, and his superlative comic genius.

Of Alfieri's twenty-two tragedies, three only are modern, and of these three the scene of one is in Spain.

Of the nine or ten tragedies of the foremost German dramatic poet, Schiller, three are German, "The Robbers," "Intrigue and Love," and "Wallenstein."

Goethe's highest dramas, "Iphigenia," "Egmont," "Torquato Tasso," are all foreign in clothing. "The Natural Daughter" has no local habitation, no dependence on time or place. "Goetz von Berlichingen," written in Goethe's earliest days of authorship, is German and in prose. "Faust" — the greatest poem of these latter times, and rivaling the greatest poems of all time — "Faust" is not strictly a drama: its wonderful successive scenes are not bound together by dramatic necessity.

The drama of Spain, like the comedies of Molière, is an exception to the rule we deduce from the practice of other dramatists ; but it is an exception which, like that of Molière, confirms the rule. Unlike the ancient Greek and the French tragic poets, unlike Schiller, Shakespeare, Goethe, Alfieri, the Spanish dramatists do not aim at ideal humanity. The best of them, Calderon, is so intensely Spanish and Romish, as to be, in comparison with the breadth and universality of his eminent compeers above named, almost provincial. His personages are not large and deep enough to be representative. The manifold recesses of great minds he does not unveil ; he gets no deeper than the semi-barbarous exaggerations of selfish, passionate love ; of revenge, honor, and jealousy. His characterization is weak. His highest characters lack intellectual calibre, and are exhibited in lyrical one-sidedness rather than dramatic many-sidedness. He is mostly content with Spanish cavaliers of the seventeenth century, ruled by the conventionalisms in manners, morals, and superstition, which have already passed away even in Spain. He is a marvelously fertile, skillful, poetic playwright.

Thus we perceive that, with poetic dramatists, the prevailing practice is, to look abroad for fables. Moreover, in the cases where these were drawn from the bosom of the poet's own people, he shuns the present, and hies as far back as he can into the dark abysms of time, as Shakespeare does in Macbeth and Lear. The Greek tragic poets, having no outward resource, took possession of the fabulous era of Greece. The poetic dramatist seeks mostly a double remoteness, that of place as well as that of time; and he must have one or the other.

The law lying behind this phenomenon is transparent. The higher poetry is, the more generic it is. Its universality is a chief constituent of its excellence. The drama is the most generically human, and, therefore, the highest of the great forms of poetry. The epic deals with the material, the outward — humanity concreted into events; the lyric with the inward, when that is so individual and intense as to gush out in ode or song. The dramatic is the union of the epic and lyric — the inward moulding the outward, predominant over the outward while co-working with it. In the dramatic, the action is more made by the personality; in the epic, the personality is more merged in the strong, full stream of events. The lyric is the utterance of one-sided, partial (however deep and earnest) feeling, the which must be linked to other feelings to give wholeness to the man and his actions. The dramatic combines several lyrics with the epic. Out of humanity and human action it extracts the essence. It presents men in their completest form, in warm activity, impelled thereto by strongest feelings. Hence, it must be condensed and compact, and must, for its highest display, get rid of local coloring, personal associations, and all prosaic circumscriptions. The poetic dramatist needs the highest poetic freedom, and only through this can he attain to that breadth and largeness whereof the superiority of his form admits, and which are such in Shakespeare, that in his greatest plays the whole world seems to be present as spectators and listeners.

Observe that the highest dramatic literatures belong to the two freest peoples — the Greeks and the English. A people, possessing already a large political freedom, must be capable of, and must be in the act of, vigorous, rich development, through deep inward passion and faculty, in order that its spirit shall issue in the perennial flowers of the poetic drama. The dramatic especially implies and demands variety and fullness and elevation of *personality;* and this is only possible through freedom, the attainment of which freedom implies on its side the innate fertility of nature which results in fullness and elevation.

Now in the subjective elevation of the individual, and therewith the unprecedented relative number of individuals thus elevated, herein do we exceed all other peoples. By subjective elevation I mean, liberation from the outward, downward pressure of dogmatic prescription, of imperious custom, of blindfolded tradition, of irresponsible authority. The despotic objectivity of Asia — where religion is submissiveness, and manhood is crushed by obedience — has been partially withstood in Europe. The emancipation therefrom of the Indo-Germanic race is completed in Anglo-America. Through this manifold emancipation we are to be, in all the high departments of human achievement, preeminently creative, because, while equipped with the best of the past, we are at the same time preëminently subjective; and, therefore, high literature will, with us, necessarily take the lyrical, and especially the dramatic, form.

More than our European ancestors, we mold,

each one of us, our own destiny; we have a stronger inward sense of power to unfold and elevate ourselves; we are more ready and more capable to withstand the assaults of circumstance. Here is more thoroughly embodied the true Christian principle, that out of himself is to come every man's redemption; that the favor and help of God are only to be obtained through resolute self-help, and honest, earnest struggle. In Christendom we stand alone as having above us neither the objectivity of politics nor that of the church. The light of the past we have, without its darkness. We carry little weight from the exacting past. Hence, our unexampled freedom and ease of movement which, wanting the old conventional ballast, to Europeans seems lawless and reckless. Even among ourselves, many tremble for our future, because they have little faith in humanity, and because they cannot grasp the new, grand historic phenomenon of a people possessing all the principles, practices, and trophies of civilization without its paralyzing incumbrances.

But think not, because we are less passive to destiny, we are rebellious against Deity; because we are boldly self-reliant, we are, therefore, irreligiously defiant. The freer a people is, the nearer it is to God. The more subjective it is, through acquired self-rule, the more will it harmonize with the high objectivity of absolute truth and justice. For having thrown off the capricious secondary rule of man, we shall not be the less, but the more, under the steadfast, primary rule of God; for having broken the force of human, fallible prescription, we shall the more feel and acknowledge the supremacy of flawless, divine law; for having rejected the tyranny of man's willfulness, we shall submit the more fully to the beneficent power of principle.

Our birth, growth, and continued weal, depending on large, deep principles — principles deliberately elaborated and adopted by reason, and generously embracing the whole — our life must be interpenetrated by principle, and thence our literature must embrace the widest and most human wants and aspirations of man. And thus, it will be our privilege and our glory to be then the most national in our books when we are the most universal.

IX.

USEFULNESS OF ART.

ADDRESS DELIVERED AT THE INAUGURATION OF THE RHODE ISLAND ART ASSOCIATION IN PROVIDENCE, SEPTEMBER 4, 1854.

Gentlemen of the Rhode Island Art Association: —

We are met to inaugurate an Association whose aim and end shall be the encouragement and culture of Art. A most high end — among the highest that men can attempt; an end that never can be entertained except by men of the best breed. There is no art among savages, none among barbarians. Barbarism and art are adversary terms. When men capable of civilization ascend into it, art manifests itself an inevitable accompaniment, an indispensable aid to human development. I will say further, that in a people the capacity to be cultivated involves the capacity, nay, the necessity of art. And still further, that those nations that have been or are preëminent on the earth, are preeminent in art. Nay, more, that a nation cannot attain to and maintain eminence without being proficient in art; and that to abstract from a people its artists were not merely to pluck the flowers from its branches; it were to cut off its deep roots.

Who is the artist?

He who embodies, in whatever mode, — so that they be visible or audible, and thus find entrance to the mind, — conceptions of the beautiful, is an artist. The test and characteristic of the artistic nature are superior sensibility to the beautiful. Unite to this the faculties and the will to give form to the impressions and emotions that are the fruit of this susceptibility, and you have the artist. Whether he shall embody his conception in written verse, in marble, in stone, in sound, on the canvas, that will depend on each one's individual aptitudes. Generic, common, indispensable to all is the superior sensibility to the beautiful. In this lies the essence of the artist.

The beautiful and the perfect being, if not identical, in closest consanguinity, the artist's is an important, a great function. The artist must receive into his mind, or engender in his mind's native richness, conceptions of what is most high, most perfect, most beautiful in shape or sound, in thought or feeling; and producing it before his fellow-men, appeal to their sensibility to the beautiful, to their deepest sympathies, to their capacity of being moved by the grandest and the noblest there is in man and nature. Truly, a mighty part is that of the artist.

Artists are the educators of humanity. Tutors and professors instruct princes and kings, but poets (and all genuine artists are poets) educate nations. Take from Greece Homer and Phidias, and Sophocles and Scopas, and the planner of the Parthenon, and you efface Greece from history. Wanting them, she would not have been the great Greece that we know; she would not have had the vigor of sap, the nervous vitality, to have continued to live in a remote posterity, immortal in the culture, the memories, and the gratitude of men.

So great, so far-stretching, so undying is the power of this exalted class of men, that it were hardly too much to say that had Homer and Phidias never lived, we should not be here to-day. If this be deemed extravagant, with confidence I affirm that but for the existence of the greatest artist the world has ever known,

— of him who may be called the chief educator of England, — but for Shakespeare, we assuredly should not be here to-day doing the good work we are doing.

There are probably some of this company who, like myself, having had the good fortune to be in London at the time of the world's fair, stood under that magnificent, transparent roof, trod that immense area whereon fifty thousand people moved at ease. It was a privilege, — the memory of which will last a life-time, to have been admitted into that gigantic temple of industry, there to behold in unimaginable profusion and variety the product of man's labor, intellect, and genius, gathered from the four corners of the earth into one vast, gorgeous pile, — a spectacle peerless from its mere material splendor, and from its moral significance absolutely sublime.

On entering by the chief portal into the transept, — covering in the huge oaks of Hyde Park, — the American, after wondering for a moment in the glare of the first aspect, will, with the eagerness and perhaps the vanity of his nation, — have hastened through the compartments of France, Belgium, Germany, gorgeous with color, glistening with gold. He will have hastened, hard as it was to hurry through such a show, in order to reach at once the far eastern end of the palace where a broad area had been allotted to the United States, — Jonathan, as is his wont, having helped himself largely. Great was the American's disappointment, cutting was the rebuke to his vanity; his country made no *show* at all. The samples of her industry were not outwardly brilliant. Their excellence lay in their inward power, in their wide usefulness. They were not ornaments and luxuries for the dwellings of the few, they were inventions that diffuse comforts and blessings among the many, — labor-saving machines and cheap newspapers. By the thoughtful visitor the merit of these was appreciated, as it was acknowledged in the final awards of the judges. And even in this high department where we are so eminent, owing to distance and misunderstandings, we were not adequately represented. But even if we had been, the European would have said, "This has a high value and interest; but still I find not here enough to justify the expectations entertained by this people, and by many in Europe, of the future greatness of the American Republic. These things, significant as they are,

are yet not an alphabet that can be so compounded as to write the richest page of man's history. In this present display I find not prefigured that splendid future the Americans are fond of predicting for themselves." And the American, acknowledging the force of the comment, would have turned away mortified, humbled. But he was saved any such humiliation. In the midst of that area, under that beautiful flag, day after day, week after week, month after month, from morn till night, go when he would, he beheld there a circle ever full, its vacancies supplied as soon as they were made, a circle silent with admiration, hushed by emotion, gazing at a master-piece of American art, the Greek Slave of Powers. And from that contemplation hundreds of thousands of Europeans carried away an impression of American capacity, a conviction that truly a great page is to be written by the young republic in the book of history,—a sense of American power which they could have gotten from no other source.

Our Association, gentlemen, owes its origin to the wants of industry. The moving power which has been strongest in bringing so many of us together to found an institution for the encouragement of art in Rhode Island, is the desire hereby more thoroughly to inweave the beautiful into cotton and woolen fabrics, into calicoes and delaines; to melt the beautiful into iron and brass, and copper, as well as into silver and gold; so that our manufacturers and artisans may hold their own against the competition of England and France and Germany, whereof in the two latter countries especially, schools of design have long existed, and high artists find their account in furnishing the beautiful to manufacturers.

"A low origin this for such a society, and the fruits will be without flavor. Art will not submit to be so lowered," will say some travelled dilettante, who, with book in hand, has looked by rote on the wonders of the Louvre and the Vatican; but the Creator of the universe teaches a different lesson from this observer. Not the rare lightning merely, but the daily sunlight, too; not merely the distant star-studded canopy of the earth, but also our near earth itself, has He made beautiful. He surrounds us with beauty; He envelops us in beauty. Beauty is spread out on the familiar grass, glows in the daily flower, glistens in the dew, waves in the commonest leafy branch. All about us, in infinite variety, beauty is lavished by God in sights and sounds, and odors. Now, in using the countless and multifarious substances that are put within our reach, to be by our ingenuity and contrivance wrought into materials for our protection and comfort, and pleasure, it becomes us to — it is part of his design that we shall — follow the divine example, so that in all our handiwork, as in his, there shall be beauty, so much as the nature of each product is susceptible of. That it is the final purpose of Providence that our whole life, inward and outward, shall be beautiful, and be steeped in beauty, we have evidence, in the yearnings of the best natures for the perfect, in the delight we take in the most resplendent objects of art and nature, in the ennobling thrill we feel on witnessing a beautiful deed.

By culture we can so create and multiply beauty, that all our surroundings shall be beautiful.

Can you not imagine a city of the size of this, or vastly larger, the structure of whose streets and buildings shall be made under the control of the best architectural ideas, being of various stones and marbles, and various in style and color, so that each and every one shall be either light, or graceful, or simple, or ornate, or solid, or grand, according to its purpose, and the conception of the builder; and in the midst and on the borders of the city, squares, and parks, planted with trees and flowers and freshened by streams and fountains. And when you recall the agreeable, the elevating sensation you have experienced in front of a perfect piece of architecture (still so rare), will you not readily concede that where every edifice should be beautiful, and you never walked or drove out but through streets of palaces and artistic parks, the effect on the whole population of this ever-present beauty and grandeur, would be to refine, to expand, to elevate. When we look at the architectural improvements made within a generation, in London, in Paris, in New York, we may, without being Utopians, hope for this transformation. But the full consummation of such a hope can only be brought about in unison with improvements in all the conditions and relations of life, and the diffusion of such improvements among the masses.

It is to further such diffusion that this Association has been founded. Our purpose is to meet the growing demand for beauty in all things; to bring into closer coöperation the artisan and the artist; to make universally visible and active the harmony, — I almost might say the identity, — there is between the useful and the beautiful.

Gentlemen, ever in the heart of the practical, in the very core of the useful, there is enclosed a seed of beauty ; and upon the fructification, growth, and expansion of that seed depends, — aye, absolutely depends, — the development of the practical. But for the expansion of that seed, we should have neither the plough nor the printing-press, neither shoes nor the steam engine. To that we owe silver forks as well as the electric telegraph. In no province of work or human endeavor is improvement made, is improvement possible, but by the action of that noble faculty through which we are uplifted when standing before a masterpiece of Raphael. This ceaseless seeking for a better, this unresting impulse towards the perfect, has brought the English race through a thousand years of gradual upward movement, from the narrow heptarchy, with its rude simplicity of life, up to this wide cultivated confederacy of states with its multiform opulence of life; and will yet carry us to a condition as much superior to our present as that is to the times of Alfred.

In the works of the Almighty this principle is so alive that they are radiant with beauty; and the degree of the radiance of each is often the measure of its usefulness. How beautiful is a field of golden wheat — whereby our bodies live — and the more beautiful the closer it stands and the fuller are its heads. The oak and the pine owe their majestic beauty to that which is the index of their usefulness, the solid magnitude of their trunks. The proportions which give the horse his highest symmetry of form, give him his fleetness and endurance and strength. And thus, too, with man, — his works, when best, sparkle most with this fire of the beautiful. We profit by history in proportion as it registers beautiful sayings and beautiful doings. We profit one another in every-day life in proportion as our acts, the minor as well as the greater, are vitalized by this divine essence of beauty. To the speeches of Webster, even to the most technical, this essence gives their completeness and their grandeur of proportion ; while it is this which illuminates with undying splendor the creations of Allston.

Thus, gentlemen, the aim of our Association is most noble and useful, drawing its nobleness from its high usefulness. May it so prosper, that a generation hence, thousands and tens of thousands shall look back to this the day of its inauguration with praise and thankfuness.

www.ingramcontent.com/pod-product-compliance
Lightning Source LLC
LaVergne TN
LVHW010241110826
845151LV00004B/1353